THE FLEETING YEARS:
A MOTHER'S JOURNAL

THE FLEETING YEARS

A MOTHER'S JOURNAL

LAURA PRATT

Signature
EDITIONS

First printing, May 2004
Second printing, January 2005

Cover design by Terry Gallagher/Doowah Design.
Cover photo of Laura Pratt by George Boyko.

This book was printed on Ancient Forest Friendly paper.
Printed and bound in Canada by AGMV Marquis Imprimeur.

We acknowledge the support of The Canada Council for the Arts and the Manitoba Arts Council for our publishing program.

National Library of Canada Cataloguing in Publication

Pratt, Laura, 1967-
The fleeting years : a mother's journal / Laura Pratt.

ISBN 0-921833-94-6

1. Parenthood—Anecdotes. I. Title.

PS8631.R37F44 2004 C818.6 C2004-901803-5

Signature Editions, P.O. Box 206, RPO Corydon
Winnipeg, Manitoba, R3M 3S7

To my mom and dad, who showed me the path.

To Adam, who walks it with me.

And, finally, to Kenya, Malindi, Finn and Kaikoura,
whose company along it I enjoy so much.

Contents

WAITING

Don't get me wrong. I love being pregnant. I love watching my belly undulate with baby rollovers. I love getting a seat in the subway during rush hour. I even love the waddle. But every pregnancy has a Wall of Tolerance, beyond which the mother-to-be becomes quite adamant to reclaim her body and get on with the next chapter. I hit that wall about four towns back.

By my calculations, I will be fifty-six weeks pregnant on Wednesday. I think they were just rolling out the Rubik's cube when I conceived. This, the "perpetual gestation," has trailed on for much longer than nature intended. Or so it seems.

Because, as anyone who's been through a full-term pregnancy could attest, the final excruciating weeks and days and minutes and moments of this going-to-have-a-baby deal can drag like the first slow ooze from a new bottle of ketchup.

When you're anticipating something as vast as creating an entire separate human life, it has a way of occupying your every waking thought. (And sleeping thoughts, too, if you count the dream I had last night about packing the baby up with the Christmas stuff, and not realizing it until April.) So anxious are you to get on with the business of shrieking in pain, choking down hospital food and introducing your offspring to the miracle that is BabyGap, that every little physical sensation becomes cause for alarm. Should you be tearing a track to the hospital, or at least boiling water? The fallout from that is that a minute tallies as an hour, an hour as an afternoon. And some afternoons last so long that I have to pack a lunch.

"What was that?" I hollered at my partner Adam the other night, so absorbed by a tremor of mild discomfort that fluttered through my body that it didn't occur to me that he wasn't also experiencing it. "What?" he asked, barely looking up from his paper. "I think I might be in labour," I ventured, though the twinge had already vanished. "Do you want me to time it?" he asked. But he didn't even glance at his watch. "No," I sighed. I have cried wolf so often with this pregnancy that even the sheep have stopped listening.

All the flat surfaces in my house are littered with scraps of paper with time notations scribbled on them. 10:23. 10:28. 10:33. Every five minutes! But then: 11:15. 12:53. And nothing more. We fell asleep on that one, my efforts to will another contraction notwithstanding. And then the next day, they pick up again: 7:12, 7:34, 8:19. Eventually, they peter out, too. And so does our conviction that we're ever going to have a baby.

Honestly, we've lost faith. Is this a contraction or is it gas? Am I even pregnant or have I just skipped a few periods and taken too many trips to the Tim Horton's drive-through? On one level, I think we both fear that this baby will never come. I will carry this kid under my shirt until he's paying off the last of his student loans, and I'm learning needlecraft at the home.

If I hear, "Are you still here?" from my next-door neighbour one more time, I may well bludgeon her. And I'm sick and tired, too, of my doctor saying, "Any minute now. I wouldn't be surprised if I see you back here tonight." But he doesn't. In fact we don't meet again until my regular appointment the next week, me the size of a Hyundai, sheepishly hauling myself — yet again — up onto the paper-covered exam bed.

Realistically speaking, I know this baby will come. I know one of these peculiar pains that washes over me will be the real thing. Talk to me then and you'll hear a different tune. Because when the big moment does arrive — along with the realization that I'm actually about to have a tiny human being to care for — it will be all I can do to slow the whole thing down.

OUR BEAN SPROUT(S)

My daughter's emergence into this world was as gradual and painstaking as our efforts to create her had been.

Adam and I called her Bean, because that is what she'd looked like in our earliest ultrasound. A lima bean, dangling inside a cavern. When I was eleven days from my due date, I realized I hadn't felt Bean move in a while. I was desperate not to be a panicky mother-to-be, showing up at my doctor's door at every twinge and hiccup. But I was genuinely concerned at this turn of events, and was starving for some peace of mind. And so I called him.

The ultrasound on the Monday revealed a vibrant, active baby. But her amniotic fluid levels were low. What's more, the doctor was concerned about her size, and suggested that it might be a good idea to induce delivery, lest she become too big to take the usual route out. We scheduled an induction for Wednesday night.

For the next two days, we survived on adrenaline and takeout. But by the time we left for the hospital on Wednesday night, me wearing the silver dolphin bracelet Adam had given me to commemorate our baby's birth, I felt calm.

In the bed across from us in triage there was a young woman in for her fifth application of gel to induce labour. That was eye-opening. We'd had visions of me going into instant fits of screaming pain as soon as the doctor approached, his gloved hands smeared with magical goo. Instead, we went home that night, watched *Beverly*

Hills 90210 and the next morning I got up with nary a cramp. I was still vastly pregnant, and we were still just a family of two.

We returned to the hospital at 8:00 am, and confirmed that, indeed, I'd made precisely no progress overnight. This time, the doctor pulled out the big guns: a stronger gel that would do more than ripen the cervix; it would stimulate labour. It worked. By 9:30, driving home in the car, I started to have contractions. It was surreal. After nine months of waiting and wondering and dreading, I was *in labour*. By 12:30, the contractions had taken on a pattern, and so we headed back to the hospital to have our baby.

After that, things unfolded in slow motion. We walked the halls, placed update phone calls and generally lived from doctor's visit to doctor's visit, to hear news of our very gradual progression. Eventually, they started me on an oxytocin drip and broke my membranes. In response, the contractions took on the characteristics of a small freight train ripping through the rocky interior caverns of my viscera (the nurse's disparaging characterization of them as "cramps" notwithstanding). Adam was wonderful, breathing and moaning and yelling right along with me. He brought me ice chips and water, and called my parents regularly and faithfully. I loved him more than ever during those dark, dark hours.

At 9:00 pm I could stand it no longer: I asked for an epidural. The hour and a half it took the anesthesiologist to get there was the most painful chunk of time I've ever endured. The key, I realized sometime into the process, was to never, ever let your mind wander to the next contraction and the jagged river of contractions that lay ahead. That would break you for sure. You had to concentrate all your energies on getting up the crest of the wave and then slipping down the other side. But it was a brutal ride. I threw up, just as I had known I would. And I ended each contraction in mortal fear of the next. At one point, I turned to Adam and said, "She's going to be an only child." I know it sounds flip now, but I really meant it. I genuinely believed that I could never, ever endure that kind of pain again in my life.

The relief of the epidural wasn't immediate, but its dilatory arrival was much appreciated. Slowly, the torture I'd been toughing out for seven hours subsided. But there were new concerns. The doctor found meconium in my waters, and it looked increasingly likely that I would have a Caesarean. And when he discovered that the baby's heart rate was dipping, and that her head was moulding too much, he told me again that emergency surgery was likely. We called my parents and gave them the news.

In the end, though, things turned on a dime. And when the nurse announced that I was ten centimetres dilated and the baby was ready to be delivered, we had to ask her to repeat it.

Right from the first push, the head appeared. "I can see her hair!" Adam shouted. I asked them to drag the big mirror over so I could watch, too. A few more pushes, and Bean's big head was lodged, partway in, partway out of me. After such a long wait, she was coming too fast. "Hold on," the doctor said. I threw up again. But I held on.

At last, my daughter arrived. She slid out of me with a rush, and the professionals closed in around her to suction her clean. And then the doctor held up my perfect little baby and said, "It's a..." But he didn't finish. Instead, he put her down on my chest for me to figure out for myself. A girl, a perfect, pink baby girl. "Let's do it again," I said to Adam.

In the end, little Kenya Lee was not so big at all: just eight pounds even. She was twenty inches long and had Apgars of eight, nine and nine. She had a full head of dark hair, funny blue eyes and a tendency to make scrunched-up faces that looked like precious smiles. And now she's here beside me, all of six days old. I am a mother. Becoming one was the hardest — and the easiest — thing I've ever done.

READJUSTMENTS

I thought I had everything mapped out. I thought I could slip a baby into my life, and have it all: the job, the family, the entire package. A rude awakening was not in the plans.

Baby Kenya is three months old. Every day is a new adventure with her, and waking up to her flapping arms and brightening face is a constant joy. But today contained no joy at all. I felt like such a terrible failure, and I wish my daughter could fast forward twenty years, so she could genuinely appreciate the apology I made to her this afternoon.

I've always been a person who couldn't sit still. Even when I was a little girl, I was textbook Type A. I had to colour inside the lines like a master, work three numbers ahead of everyone else on the multiplication tables and make a successful living from an entrepreneurial venture drawing people's caricatures at a sidewalk table after school.

When I decided to have children, I embraced the idea with the same enthusiasm as I do everything. It would be great, I fantasized. Like having a little doll to play with when I wasn't busy working. I gave precious little thought to having to alter my schedule in order that I might accommodate the change. After all, little babies sleep an awful lot. I would nurse her while typing; and then I would set her down in her car seat and continue to work. It was an idyllic plan that left me entirely unprepared for the reality of my first child.

Yesterday, when I was still full of hope, I scheduled an interview for 3:00 this afternoon. Surely Kenya would be napping then, I thought. Everything would go off without a hitch. But Kenya wasn't napping at 3:00, nor was she at 4:00 (the time for which I had frantically rescheduled the conversation). I tried to make the call anyway, arranging my daughter on a blanket under her hanging bear gym on my office floor. But she got cranky before I had even finished dialing the numbers, and I had to turn my attention entirely to her.

She was inconsolable.

Eventually, I bailed on the interview altogether, and put Kenya in the living-room swing so I could make myself a sandwich. But I was so flustered that I didn't properly belt her in, and she slipped out and dropped onto the carpet as soon as I left for the kitchen. I felt awful, and more frustrated by my thwarted plans than ever. It was then that I decided I had to teach my little sweetheart that she couldn't expect to be held all of the time. Her mother had a life besides her, after all. And she wasn't prepared to shut the door on it.

It's so hard to know what's the right thing to do when you're a mommy. You never, ever want to make your baby feel that you're not there for her, but then everyone warns you that you're spoiling the child and making her too dependent if you answer her every call.

And so it was on this day that I put baby Kenya in her crib with her mobile turning above her and came into my office and slipped a music CD into the computer. This was so I wouldn't hear my beautiful little princess's wails coming from the next room. This was so I wouldn't be exposed to my child's pain as she learned that she could not be the centre of her mother's attention all of the time.

It was the most awful thing in the world.

When I finally came in to rescue my child — to whom I promised to dedicate all of my attention from that moment on — she was all out of breath with her desperate little cries. And I had to cry too. No job is that important, I realized. Nothing is. And while I'm aware that things have got to change now, if I plan to keep on working, I've got the satisfaction of knowing my priorities are straight at last.

To Kenya, at Six Months

I remember you, my little six-month-old thing, when you were nothing more than a heartbeat. A tiny miner's hammer tap-tap-tapping away, wetly, in a distant mine.

And then you were a blurry picture, partly mysterious, partly delightfully identifiable. You were tucked up there, inside my tummy, sucking your thumb.

And then here you were. After such a long, long time, and suddenly, both at once. Imagine.

After cleaning you off, they handed you up to me, just like they do in the movies. For a fraction of a second you lay, squirming, wet, slippery, on my chest — and I panicked. I didn't know what to do with you. I was scared to touch you. Surely I'd infect you. You were perfect. Pure. Untouched by the world. But then I put my hands on your flawless little body and I knew it was going to be all right.

That night, my baby, I slept with you in my arms, breathing in your hair. It was the sweetest sleep I'd ever known.

I can't believe half a year has passed since you came into our lives. Life before you is just a vague memory now, like a movie I've mostly forgotten the plot of. It's been the greatest pleasure and sharpest sadness watching you grow, little girl, into who you are today. My dadadadada quacking duck. Bright and alert. Full of smiles for the world. A bag of perfumed breath and baby wheezes, sleeping on my chest every night.

To think, someday you'll no longer be this small. With each passing day you need me a little less. Your world expands. Truly, I'm happy for you, but the ironic dual nature of a mother's love sometimes threatens to tear me apart.

Tonight, you are sleeping, wrapped in a red sleeper that's in danger of being tossed in your too-small pile, and your favourite cow blanket. I should be sleeping too, because the cumulative sleep loss has caught up with me terribly. But I'm in my office, thinking of you, as I often do. I look up at the newborn picture I've taped to the top of my computer and think about how you're just a flower, really, whose petals, all folded in when you arrived, are unfolding a little more each day to reveal the person you will become.

I love you, my Kenya Lee. With a new, unfamiliar love that reaches the roots of my being. I know someday my flower will head off for her own garden. It's a thought too sad to bear. My only comfort is my commitment to spend the rest of my days filling my senses with your progressive bloom.

FIRST BIRTHDAY

Behind me, in a yellow room we prepared for a person we did not know, my one-year-old baby sleeps. She wheezes slightly, and occasionally snorts. Her head is full of dreams. Dreams that get bigger as time goes by.

For the first little while, I was all that she had. But every day now, she has more. I know today people will tell me that she's not my baby anymore. That she's now a little girl. And that's OK. But it's so, so hard to let go.

I didn't know what it would be like to be a mother to this little child. What business did I have being a parent? I was just a kid myself. But one year in, I feel much more confident. Nothing gives me greater joy than hauling my daughter up onto my lap or hearing her sing out Mamama when I come into sight. Her smiles light up the room. And her sweetness could ice the birthday cake Mommy made a mess of in the kitchen. She is my greatest treasure, and I am so grateful for how her presence has taught me what really matters.

Today, my baby is one. A year suddenly means so much more, now that I have her to mark it for me. Everything resonates from this time last year. I remember being totally dumbstruck to be entirely responsible for another human life. OK, what happens now? I remember thinking, that first night home. I wanted so very, very much for my child. But I had no idea where to begin.

Now I know it comes in steps. And Kenya and I have only just begun our marathon.

Every night, when I lay my baby down in her crib, tuck her blankets around her in our special way, give her Goofy to hug in her arms, turn on her lullaby tape and tell her I love her, I always think how special the moment is. It's never, ever routine, because I'm all too aware that it's a sweetness that's fleeting. All too soon, Kenya will be two. And then four. And then fourteen. My role will diminish, and her world will open up. And so I'm always thinking — always thinking — how wonderful, how special, how poignant our moments are.

PUBLIC PROPERTY

I'm newly pregnant, and on the subway, holding a post and swaying with the motion of the ride. "I'll bet you've got gas," an older woman in a Casino Rama T-shirt says sympathetically, as she stands to give me her seat. I tell her thank you and pray she doesn't pursue that train of thought. Of course she does, and I briefly travel with it, confessing that my pregnant state has made me no more gaseous than usual. Mercifully, her stop arrives and I'm left to marvel at how a pregnancy opens a person up for public consumption. "Can I touch it?" strangers will ask, their hands already pressing against my belly. If they know me well, they might inquire as to the likelihood of my peeing my pants if they tell a joke that makes me howl, or of having a bowel movement while delivering the baby.

I had wild morning sickness with my last pregnancy and had occasion more than once to lose my lunch in public view. One time, I threw up in a downtown alleyway as handsome couples, en route from the parking lot to various fancy dining establishments, recoiled in horror.

Another time, I was in the car when the urge washed over me like so much undigested corn. Having recently cleared the vehicle of all errant fast-food paraphernalia, I was left with no option but to pull the vehicle over and vomit into the cupholders in the middle console. The mothers lining the sidewalk were thus treated to my take on one of the messier pleasures of pregnancy.

But it got worse. Because let's face it, the indignities of a pregnancy are a walk in the park compared with the humiliation enjoyed by a woman during those grueling minutes and hours when she's giving birth. Legs flung wide apart, she is the hostess with the mostest as she entertains a parade of visitors who wander in and out of the scene, her exposed views notwithstanding. Indeed, the lady of the hour generally laughs gaily with her hospital-room guests, and takes various stabs at small talk, all the while trying to forget their perspective on her situation. "Is it any warmer outside?" she might ask, above the snap of a rubber glove. And someone might answer, "Nope. Still too cool for golf," with his hand deep inside her, and his medical student gazing over his shoulder at the action. Lack of eye contact is forgiven during these proceedings.

Then, before you know it, you're pushing your baby into the arms of some guy who hasn't even bought you dinner, and it's over. Your pregnancy's a thing of the past, and you're just one more invisible member of the population. Best of all: your gastrointestinal activities are once more no one's business but your own.

To Kenya, at Age Two

Dear little Kenya Lee,

Two years is a very, very long time. Indeed, it's your whole life. What a remarkable evolution you've undergone in that span. From a wriggling, slippery pink bantling to a human being in miniature.

No one can believe you're just two. Your conversation is too sophisticated, your level of understanding too great. Of course, a mother's viewpoint is a wee bit biased and I must be forgiven for expanding your seeds of praise into entire orchards. You speak like a pro, and I observe the machinations of your clever little mind behind every statement you make. You're a thoughtful, reasonable person. Outbursts for you are rare. You seem to accept the limitations of your existence and, although you're a saucy contrarian from time to time, you generally come around with a bit of on-the-level explanation.

What you know and who you are astounds me. You hear so much and you store it away. You're curious, but understand risk. You love to laugh and possess a cultivated appreciation of the importance of a good sense of humour. And you're a sensitive little thing, who cries when her mommy cries and are the first to rush forth with a head-cocked *You OK?* after the crisis passes. All of these qualities, my love, will serve you well.

Dear, sweet Kenya Lee, you are my most powerful force. You are my unwavering light, the roots of my tree, my constant joy. You've expanded my world and focused my purpose. I know when I read this when you're five or fifteen, I'll search between the lines for a sense of who you were when you were just two — but now you just are. Squealing with laughter. Frothing with demands. Singing self-conscious songs. Racing down the hallway, all bare bum and badness. I will always remember you like this, I tell myself. But of course I won't.

Soon, you will have a brother or sister. I wonder how you will react, my little one, to having to share your precious spotlight. I take heart in knowing the companion we provide for you will outlast our company and serve as your mirror, your bouncing-off surface, your co-conspirator and the bearer of half your misery. But, in the beginning, he or she will almost certainly be the source of nothing but jealousy.

It makes me profoundly sad to realize our time together is about to be dramatically altered. Our privacy is going to be invaded; our rituals changed. Soon a family of four will be all you remember, and what you've known up till now will slip past the grasp of your memory. I will never forget the magic of our cozy trio though, my dear. One day, I will tell you stories about how wonderful it was.

WELCOME, MALINDI

Baby Malindi lies beside me now, a peeping, wiggly package of newborn. I feel like I've known her forever, as she made her physical self felt so long ago inside me; and yet, she's still such a stranger.

A second baby is not at all like the first. Because of the passage you've already been through, it's impossible not to impose expectations and interpretations on the subsequent child. For all her newness, Malindi has been done before, in the form of Kenya. All of which makes her that much less surprising, that much less intimidating — but no less joyful.

Malindi came into the world at her own pace. I felt like she was overdue long before she was. Too many close calls with the likes of placenta previa, prolapsed cords and toxemia made me believe she would arrive sooner than she did. It's probably what brought me to the hospital last week, certain I was experiencing some of the dangerous side symptoms of high blood pressure. I had a headache, or at least I imagined I did. And I thought my vision might be a bit blurred, but perhaps my contacts were just dry. At any rate, we dropped Kenya with my parents and headed to the hospital. In the end, my blood pressure was deemed within healthy confines for the first time in four weeks, my urine was clear, and, lo, my vision had apparently sharpened up. They sent me home.

Two nights later, we were back.

Weary of recording every stitch as a possible start to labour, I had decided to take Kenya to a movie. We availed ourselves of an enormous bucket of popcorn and settled down in front of a parrot's tale of mishap and folly, me doing my best to ignore the muscular activities of my uterus throughout the drama. But the second the closing credits started to roll, I grabbed my two-year-old's hand and raced out of the theatre. "I think I'm in labour!" I hollered up the stairs to Adam when we threw open the front door of our house. Then it was off to the hospital, Part Two.

All the way there, my contractions got stronger. Honestly. Even in the parking lot I had to stop a moment to sweat out a particularly painful one. But by the time the ladies in white had me in a bed and strapped up to a monitor, the contractions had fizzled out all together.

The nurses would occasionally come and eye my readout, ask solicitously whether I'd had any contractions (when the unswerving lines clearly revealed I hadn't) and wander away to chuckle about me in the breakroom (or so I believed). Eventually, a doctor came in and did an internal, which showed that I was still stuck at two centimetres. I returned home with my tail — and precious little else — between my legs.

Everyone on our street, it turned out, had been alerted to my labouring state. Imagine their surprise when they saw me hopping out of the Honda, as pregnant as ever.

Fast forward to Part Three.

Two days later, I woke up early with cramps that I didn't dare imagine to be contractions. We went to a movie that afternoon, and then met up with friends. I never mentioned to a soul the possibility that I might be in labour. Back at home, we played Monopoly, and then went to my parents' house for Sunday dinner. By dessert, I had no doubt.

This time, the nurses on the maternity floor gave me smiles of legitimacy as I shuffled into their midst, in obvious pain. But it wasn't long before an air of dubiousness fell over the place. Again, my contractions (one nurse referred to them as "prelabour symptoms") slowed once they put the monitors on me. They sent me home.

But Adam and I had had enough. I knew I was in labour and we weren't about to head all the way back to our house, only to have to turn around in an hour. So we scouted out hotels in the downtown core. Once ensconced in a $200-a-night room too far from the elevators for a labouring woman, we ordered room service (Adam had an all-day breakfast and a piece of chocolate cake; I had a club sandwich) and switched on *The Larry Sanders Show.* Each time I contracted, I insisted on having the sound muted. Adam would try to lip-read the punchlines while stroking my arm. We stayed for just over two hours, riding the contractions until I could stand it no longer.

The bellboy who came to help us with our stuff was the first of the alarmed hotel staffers we met on our journey down to the taxi. First, he wanted to hold my hand. Then he got our bag stuck in the elevator door. Down in the lobby, the manager hollered at various employees for not calling an ambulance for me. Then he offered to pay for our cab and hurried me out so I wouldn't deliver a baby on his carpet.

Back at the hospital, my labour was confirmed: I was four centimetres and in so much pain I thought I was going to expire. The tough British nurse Maggie was full of praise for how I was getting through, and I know she was angling for me to forego the epidural. But I called for the anesthesiologist anyway and, more than an hour later, the blessed man arrived.

Afterwards, Maggie set up a bed for Adam, and both of us settled down for some sleep. Morning dawned slowly, and my epidural wore off just as I reached ten centimetres. My doctor came in and announced that the head was down and had turned (she'd been facing the wrong direction). I only pushed three times before a squirming blue being slipped out onto the bloody sheets between my legs.

They forgot to tell me the sex of my new baby, and Adam saw me struggling to see. She's a girl, he said. Then they put her on my chest and I felt so much more at ease with her than I had with my new Kenya. Hello, sweetheart, I said. And then they took Malindi Kia away to prepare her for greeting the world.

THE SECOND CHILD

Why is it, my lovely Malindi, when I walk into the bedroom you now share with your big sister to gaze upon your splayed-open wonder in the night, that I feel sorrow? Why do I feel a lump rise in my throat as I watch your blossom lips work in dreamed suckings and listen to your gulps of infant sleep? Why does each day pass for me with the knowledge that another is gone rather than that another will soon be upon us?

Perhaps that is the curse of the second child, my love. The miracle of your sister has taught me just how swiftly this time does pass, more so than any words of warning from other moms ever could. Now you are three months old and your sister is almost three years. In her face, I still sometimes see the infant she was, but she's mostly girl now. Soon you will be there, too, giggling like a bird, struggling to understand the emerging world.

But for now you're still my precious baby. Still my little lamb, with fat folds of thighs and a radiant smile which lights up the night sky with its absolutely unabashed expression of delight. Life will never be this pure for you again, never this simple, never this focused.

When people tell me you're getting so big, I feel the swelling of an ache and I want to tell them (and sometimes do) that that couldn't possibly be the case. Why, only three months ago you were still a part of my body, sharing my every movement and breath. Surely you're still the tiny infant I cradled in my hospital room.

But here you are, trying on the world for size, swimming across the bed on your back when I'm not looking, kicking your legs like an athlete as I support your sweet peanut head in the bathtub. You seem a happy little cherub, so far. Perhaps we're all a little less frantic the second time around. And if we don't jump at your first little cries, it's only because we've learned we don't have to — not because we love you any less.

And if you are my last, a thought that crosses my consciousness darkly more often than I care to admit, then I must cup my hands together and drink up every moment of you like water. But of course the water drains through the cracks, and the constant scooping becomes exhausting. In the end, I will let you grow, my love — both up and away. What other choice do I have?

TO KENYA, AT AGE THREE

My dear, sweet Kenya,

Yes, I'm late. Your third birthday came and went a month ago. But I'm a mommy to two now, and time is a luxury. Particularly since you've become so obsessed with play-acting, and on insisting that your parents play the roles in the many dramas that consume your little life. I hear you in your bedroom now, giggling with your daddy, insisting that he's "the 'laddin." You, of course, are Jasmine.

Or Beauty. Or Kiara. Always the princess. Always the best parts. Sometimes, you'll tease me: "Who do you want to be, Mommy" (the first question in the morning; the last at night), "Esmerelda, or Quasimodo?" "Esmerelda," I'll say, with enthusiastic delight, only to have the assignment snatched away from me. "No! I'm Esmerelda," you'll say. "You be Quasimodo." You are the consummate director. The brightest star.

Suddenly, without warning, you're three. The days and weeks have roared past and now I can scarcely remember the little bag of baby love I wrote about in my missives to an earlier version of you. Now you're a true little girl, fascinated with the girly things I'd always hoped my daughter would be: tucking dollies into bed, building castles for your figurines to marry in, wearing a tiara into the bath.

Last night, I snuck into your room, all aglow with the coloured Christmas lights I'd strung around your window, and freed your feet from the duvet to cool you. Such little feet, I thought, and I spent a moment gazing at their perfection, marvelling at the fireball of energy for which they provide a base. Then I kissed them, and peeled your sticky hair back from your face, and left the room. You slept all night after that, as you've been so often doing these days. It took three years, but I think I can finally join the ranks of mommies who crow that their babies "sleep through the night." It was touch and go there for a while, my love. But I think you've been worth it.

Now that there's a little sister on the scene, six months old and your biggest fan, I have some context in which to place you. No matter how long I look at your baby photos, downy hair fanned over your head, dimpled fingers reaching for toys, you're forever three in my mind. You've always been showing off to your friends, always insisting on games of hide and seek during which you almost always hide in the same spot. But the baby-ness of Malindi's life reminds me of just how far you've come.

Sometimes, I must confess, I forget how much further there is to go. I speak to you as an adult, and expect adult behaviour in response. When you dissolve into the sillies, or into tears, I'm reminded that you are, after all, only three years old.

You're such a funny little creature, my darling, and I wish I could imprint forever all your quirkiness and cleverness on my brain. The way you're so solemn at the amusement park, or whenever anyone's snapping a picture of you. The way you insist on dresses, because that's what Cinderella or Esmerelda would wear. The way you "do angry" when I brush your front teeth. The way you ask us to stay with you in bed at night "for just a couple minutes, and then go."

But, alas, you're a moving target. It scares me to think that, in time, my memories of you as a three-year-old will also be foreign and out of reach. But I love the way you're growing, my freckle-nosed, big-eyed drama queen. You fill me with pride with your observations and your sweet nature. I'll never forget the night Mommy was sad, and you carefully lifted her hair out of her eyes and said, "That will feel better." So I asked you then, as I do every night, "What's in there?" And you put your hand on my hand, resting on your chest, and smiled. "Heart."

You got it, lover.

LOST TREASURES

We got to the hospital at 6:45 this morning. We dressed Kenya in hospital pyjamas and tied up her hair. The hospital staff weighed her and gave her an identification bracelet. We went over the content of our disclosure forms with a couple of different people. And then they whisked my little girl, clutching her stuffed hippo (who was also assigned a hospital identification bracelet) away for dental surgery. We were left on the other side of the swinging doors, to wait and to worry.

A hundred years later, the dentist came out to the dim parents' lounge, and Adam and I flipped shut our out-of-date magazines and sat upright on the vinyl furniture to hear her report. I could tell by the look in her eyes that she had something important to say. She did. In addition to filling myriad cavities, they had discovered such advanced decay in Kenya's two front teeth, she told us, that they'd had no choice but to pull them. For a moment, there was silence. And then I gulped some air and asked the dentist to please say it again.

Nobody had mentioned anything about extractions. And we had no idea that there were problems with the front teeth at all. I know the dentist could have been telling us something much, much worse. But my little girl's baby teeth were gone forever and that's all I could think about. They handed me a little plastic treasure chest containing my sweetheart's lost treasures. But there was no way I could open it and look inside.

At last, we were called to the recovery room. When they wheeled her in on a gurney, my little daughter had just begun to cry. Her throat hurt, because she'd been intubated. And she really wanted a drink. Her lips were all swollen and stained with blood. She looked so tiny — but with such big, big eyes.

"Mommy, I just want to cuddle up with you," Kenya said. I wrapped my arms around her, as best I could across the railings of her bed, and she slept for a bit. And then she started throwing up, mostly blood. Adam and I were both freaked out, but they assured us it was normal.

And now we're home. We've gone through several pairs of pyjamas and literally all of the blankets in the house. If she throws up again, I'm going out to buy another comforter. Kenya's alternately happy and bubbly (although she's not allowed to even walk today) and very low key and flat. Her smile without front teeth is silly. But sad. And two years too soon. I hope the other kids don't tease her.

I love my sweet, lovely Kenya, toothless though she may be, and I thank God she came through this OK. What are two teeth anyway? Besides, now we know what she wants for Christmas.

Pregnant Sex

I'm pregnant again. It was neither planned nor unplanned. Adam and I are both coming to terms with it in our own way. His greatest fear, at least for the moment, is about what kind of impact this development will have on our sex life.

In one sense, having sex when you're pregnant is a bit counterproductive. Let's face it: the horse is already out of the barn. The deed is done and you have the blistering nipples to prove it. On the other hand, it might just be human nature to want to return to the scene of your last great success and try to duplicate it. Either way, there's no denying that having a gestating fetus along for the ride does its bit to change the dynamics of a couple's sexual relationship.

I have a friend who sums the whole issue of sex and pregnancy up this way: There isn't much that's less appealing than a guy who gets his kicks out of fooling around with a woman who's twice his size and a lot more grouchy. She is definitely in the camp of women whose nine-month modus operandi is to regard their partner's sexual equipment like the big box of maxipads in the cupboard: something they won't be needing for a while. Sex, for these folks, is just one more burden on an increasingly demanding schedule.

Don't get me wrong. There's definitely something to be said for pregnant sex. After too many years of worrying what might happen if the condom broke, well, what's broke is broke at this point, and nobody's fretting about getting anything fixed. What's more, there's a slew of physiologic evidence to suggest that women are never more receptive to sexual congress than when they're bulging with child. Various things are swollen beyond their normal size, and blood is coursing through the nether regions like it's powered by some internal pump. Proof positive of this is another friend who practically erected a full-size gym in her bedroom during her two pregnancies to contain her sexual energy. I was way into it, she enthuses. It was like I was twice taken over by some demon goddess of sex. My husband couldn't keep up.

And speaking of husbands keeping things up, they've got their camps on this issue, too. For some, a pregnant woman is a ripe fruit, just asking to be plucked from the tree and devoured. For others, she is Mother Nature herself, and there's no messing with that kind of perfection. Besides, these men might protest, what's the baby going to think, getting poked at up in there? To them, I say: If you imagine your dipstick has that kind of reach, you're engaging in some wishful thinking indeed. But I digress.

For me, sex and pregnancy are like flirtatious old friends, occasionally getting silly and falling into bed together, sometimes realizing the wisdom of keeping a distance. At some points in my pregnancies, I couldn't get enough of the stuff. I was just so tickled by my inflated sense of self that I had to share the wealth. Then, near the end, there were the physical improbabilities of the whole affair that I couldn't get over. And it really did start to feel like our kid was witnessing something — albeit with an interior view — that could put her in therapy twenty years hence.

And so sex with my partner invariably slows to a crawl when I am with child. In turn, the tension in the house starts to swell like some vast occupied uterus. But, soon enough, the baby arrives, and we can resume our regular schedule of twice-nightly romps in the hay. I am, of course, joking. Because if you think pregnancy has a role to play in a man and woman's sex life, well, you ain't seen nothing yet.

KENYA'S FIRST DAY

Dear Kenya,

Tomorrow afternoon you will be in a classroom, beginning your very first day of kindergarten.

It doesn't seem that long ago that school was eons away. The big kids who trudged back and forth along the sidewalks in front of our house, eating their sandwiches and knocking against our garbage cans, may as well have been different species. And now here it is upon us.

My heart clenches when I imagine you there, out in the world. A real little person. But still so small. A tiny green-eyed moppet dwarfed by the knapsack on her back. How will they treat you? How will you be received?

To me, school was a grand adventure. But it was fraught with perils. Little kids can be so, so cruel. I don't want them to crush my little flower, or even sully her perfect petals. But I know that's too much to ask. I know that you are embarking on an excursion that will see you teased. Excluded. Hurt. And when you look around for your mommy, she will be nowhere in sight.

You'll learn, though, to comfort yourself. To patch up your own scrapes. To cope. And I will always, always be there, just blocks away, waiting breathlessly to hear about your day.

You're on your own now, my love. At least for a couple of hours every afternoon. But it's the beginning of a very long journey that will consume you for the next two decades or more. In spirit, I will always be there beside you. Holding your little hand. Brushing your hair out of your eyes. Whispering into your ear. You were my first, my love. The first to arrive in my life. And the first to take baby steps away from it.

You leave me in your dust, sweet girl, as you enter into this other place. This place where the world, once limited to a mommy's hovering presence alone, will rise up around your little shoulders. Who knew there was so much out there?

Welcome to it, my sweet. I know you will be fascinated. I know there will be days when you'll rush home to me with huge eyes to talk about coloured-pencil maps and seedlings sprouting from glass jars. I'm so excited for you. Now I just have to get over this hump. I need to let my own little seedling sprout from her glass jar and trail into her own garden.

I love you, sweet Kenya. I'll miss you, from 12:55 until 3:20 every single day. I'll think of you, earnest and quiet, sitting in a circle with your peers, soaking up all of that good stuff kindergarten's going to share with you. I had a wonderful three years and ten months and five days with you all to myself. And now I'll loose you, as much as it pains me to do so, onto the next stage.

Be kind, my dear. Always think before you speak. Don't be a bossy-boots. Befriend the little kid that others have cast out. Be your own person. Think your own thoughts. Be polite. Share your stuff. Watch where you're going. Listen — and then talk. Don't run too fast. Try as hard as you can. Be proud, but not vain. And enjoy.

Goodbye, little one. And good luck.

ELECTRONIC FRIENDSHIPS

It was more than four years ago that I made my first acquaintance with a dozen of my closest friends. Of course, we had no idea then what would come of our casual meeting on this cool new thing called the Internet. We simply stumbled across one another on a newsgroup, all of us newly pregnant, all seeking advice for the sea change our lives were about to undergo, none of us particularly in the market for lifelong buds. At some point, someone suggested that the women due in the same two-month period break off into a subgroup, which we did. And we've never looked back.

The October-November list, as we've come to call ourselves, is now populated with about eighty active members, all of us with four- or nearly four-year-olds. Most are American, though there are half a dozen Canadians, an Aussie and a mother of four who lives in Israel. Some are stay-at-home moms; the rest are employed in a range of professional pursuits. There's a millionaire on our list. A cowboy's wife. A couple of lawyers' wives. Two of our children are adopted. One is autistic.

We "talk" about everything under the sun. Some of our more recent topics of discussion have included musings on how many shoes each of us has in her closet, how to make impossible cheeseburger pie, how to help your kid to focus in the classroom and how to get nail polish off your computer screen.

A couple of times a year, we hold "get-togethers," so that at least some of us can make personal contact. We've met in Chicago, Phoenix,

San Francisco, Washington, Las Vegas, even Toronto. These weekends are essentially big estrogen fests in which a bunch of suddenly liberated-from-their-kids mothers let loose in the big city. Not pretty.

Inevitably, a smattering of cliques has emerged from within our ranks. There's the Phoenix Ladies. The Alabama Gang. The Tree Huggers. But they don't make themselves known too often, and aren't usually exclusionary. We only realize they're out there when we launch into some political discussion or talk about incendiary stuff like whether butter should be spread on cinnamon toast before or after the toasting. When conflict occurs, though, it tends to go underground. The Civil War was refought on-line (the North won again, I think). One list member slugged it out with another's husband over the Atkins Diet, and some feathers got ruffled over that.

But more than anything, this diverse group of ladies with whom I trade several dozen e-mails a day are my friends. My support. My addiction (when our list server was in the tank recently, the withdrawal I suffered was palpable). Our kids are exactly the same age, and the ability this little arrangement has afforded us to share all manner of child-rearing crap over the years — from toilet training to training wheels — has been invaluable.

I don't think my IRL (that would be "in real life") friends fully appreciate how much my little band of Internet buds means to me. They figure that the lack of proximity and face-to-face contact means they couldn't possibly be genuine confidantes. What they don't realize is that our modern friendship is as intimate and fulfilling as its more conventional counterparts. I'm as close to many of my electronic friends as I am to the flesh-and-blood buddies I linger over my kitchen table with. Indeed, research has proven that Internet relationships are sometimes more interesting, thanks in part to the liberation the isolated activity of tapping away at a keyboard in the privacy of your home affords you. These women know stuff about me that nobody else does. And if I'm having a particularly challenging day, I won't hesitate to unload on air to the group. They care about how I'm doing. And they'll fill up my in-box to prove it.

Remember This

My dear sweet little cherub Malindi,

I must remember this.

I must remember those chocolate brown eyes, fringed with the lovely lashes I once thought would never grow long enough to distinguish you as a girl, peering up at me in mischief.

I must remember the songs you invent to celebrate everything, from bees to cars to shoes to — happily — Mommy.

I must remember your perpetual joy, the way you take pleasure from every little thing, the way you laugh with such dedication that the noise swells up from the pit of your very being.

I must remember your calmness, your reasonable embrace of almost everything ("OK, Mommy"), your peaceful little disposition.

I must remember your spinning little dances, and how you laugh so hard over them that you fall down, giggling still.

I must remember your penchant for particular footwear ("old shoes") and jammies ("La La dress") and jackets ("bee coat").

I must remember your radiant sense of humour, and the way it draws genuine laughter from me again and again and again.

I must remember the time you take to fall asleep in your crib, private time, used to invent new lyrics and to rhapsodize over the events of your day.

I must remember the way you wake up, greeting the morning under a tangled head of crazy hair, with the kind of anticipation only a two-year-old could have.

I must remember the relationship I've watched blossom between you and your sister, big eyed and watchful, loving and ultimately mysterious for the dynamic it embodies that I will never fully understand.

I must remember how very much I enjoy your company, little girl, how you're never, ever a burden, but always, always a delight.

I must remember your last summer of babyhood, your last summer of pudgy legs and rounded forehead and chubby cheeks, your last summer of a certain kind of silliness that will never come this way again. I must remember this.

I love you, my sweet second child, my precious baby girl, my Malindi.

The Bump

Girl Guides and Boy Scouts earn badges for passing certain milestones. I think parents should, too.

My pursuit of this latest badge of courage began at 5:30 this afternoon. My mom and dad were coming for dinner and Adam and I were getting stuff ready for a barbecue. Luther was at the back sliding door barking. I was in the living room at the other end of the house and there wasn't any way I was hauling ass to open the damn door with a perfectly capable four-year-old about. I shouted for Kenya to let the dog in. Next thing I knew, she was screaming.

I must admit, I didn't move too quickly. Kenya's our drama queen, and my first reaction was that she was putting on one more performance. When I reached her, I gathered her into my arms as I sat down. Through wails, she told me that she'd run into the door. "It's OK," I said. "Don't worry." And then I looked at her head.

To my amazement, there was the most incredible bump forming on her forehead. Before my eyes, it grew to the size of a golf ball. It was almost like a whole other head was taking shape above her eye. Scarred with a deep gash, it was purple all around.

I screamed for Adam, who was fortunately nearby. I know he was shocked when he saw her, but he told me to relax, which was good advice because I was starting to shake and cry. I think we were both expecting the thing to burst, swelling as it was on the left side of our daughter's skull. He grabbed *What to Expect When You're Expecting* off the bookshelf and started scouring for medical advice. I just hollered at him, "It's a pregnancy book!"

He told me to call 9-1-1. I did, and the patient person at the other end of the line, whom I could barely hear because of all the screaming (mine, not hers), asked where I lived, and what the problem was. I told her that my daughter had banged into a door and that she had a bruised bump the size of an apple rising off her forehead. She asked me if it was bleeding, and I said no. She said they would send paramedics around to take a look.

By then Adam had located a more appropriate source of reference, and was reading out loud that it's not uncommon for head injuries to result, very quickly, in bumps. It recommended a cold compress, which Adam was miraculously able to produce. Soon after that, the paramedics showed up and very efficiently took Kenya's pulse, looked in her eyes, pushed on the bruise, and asked us lots of questions about her demeanour and state of consciousness. They told us to monitor whether she appeared confused at all and to be particularly watchful if she threw up.

Half an hour later, just as Adam was putting the burgers on the grill, Kenya vomited.

I was so, so scared. My mom (we'd telephoned my parents right after hanging up from the paramedics) came running in and put on her shoes and said we had to go to the hospital right then. I was debating whether we should drive or call for an ambulance again. But as we were all gathering our thoughts, and washing the vomit off Kenya and her stuffed hippo, didn't the little kid just go through a complete transformation. Suddenly, she was fine, up on her feet, tripping off to watch a video, asking for something to eat. We decided to wait it out a bit longer.

A few hours along, things began to look better still. She ate a whole can of soup for dinner, along with some crackers, and then some ice cream. We never went to Emergency.

The bump has diminished, and she's been in bed for half an hour. As for me, I'm hovering, absolutely drained, breathless with relief — and waiting for my badge.

Welcome, Finn

The most frustrating thing about my son Finn's entry into the world was its uncertainty. Well, his eventual arrival was always certain. But, as was the case with his big sister Malindi, exactly when it would take place was much in question in the last days of his in-utero stay.

Officially, I choose to trace labour back to last Saturday. It was raining, and we took the family for a drive in our spanking new minivan to a restaurant on the east side of town. On the way there, and again on the way home, contractions kicked in, in a distressingly regular fashion. Every four to eight minutes. Not painful at all, but insistent. We began to be convinced that "tonight would be the night." It was the first of many such convictions.

Late that night, the contractions stopped.

Sunday, labour was sporadic. Start and stop. Start and stop. Sometimes the contractions were eight or eleven minutes apart. And then two hours would pass with nothing. On Monday, I couldn't bear another day of wondering and willing. My mom came over in the morning, and we cleaned the house like bandits. Every now and again, I would announce, "I'm having a contraction!" But nobody paid any mind to such declarations after two days of false starts.

In the afternoon, I phoned Adam to tell him "tonight might be the night." He reluctantly agreed to leave the office, and I had to work to convince him upon his arrival that these things were "real." The contractions kept up through the wee morning hours, and he called work to announce that he wouldn't be in. The day, it seemed, was finally upon us. But then, at 8:13 am, they stopped. Just like that. Flat out. I couldn't have been more depressed.

In the end, I left the girls with a babysitter, took Adam to the office, and kept on driving. I stopped at my old neighbourhood, parked the van outside my old house and walked. I walked and walked. I walked all through my old haunts, and all the way to my old school. By the time I was sitting down for lunch at a local deli, the contractions had started again. They were big enough this time to make me blanch, and to hope the waiter wouldn't drop by to check on the quality of my meal in the midst of one.

In the afternoon, I had an ultrasound, and the doctor declared me about two to three centimetres along. For good measure, he "stretched me," and I was off. On the way home, the real stuff hit. So powerful were these shuddering clutches of pain, that I actually had to pull the van to the shoulder to get through them. When I got home, I started timing. The contractions were coming every four to five minutes and were as powerful as a vise grip clenching my internal organs. I called Adam and the hospital.

The drive through rush-hour traffic back downtown was excruciating and the walk from the parking lot, which was across the street from the hospital, took twenty minutes. I was hooked up, and wearing something blue and institutional by 6:45. I asked for an epidural, and they supplied one by about 8:00 pm, which I thought was pretty impressive. Some of the contractions in the interim were awful, because Adam was downstairs giving a credit card imprint and I felt quite alone.

The pain never really dissipated, and I eventually asked the nurses for a top-up. They didn't check me first, and when the doctor came to have a peek soon after, he announced that I was ten centimetres. Adam and I looked at each other. I'm not ready, we both confessed.

By then, I was so hepped up on the epidural medicine that there was no way I could push on my own. It was strange to be so disconnected from the birth of my baby. They didn't provide a mirror for me to watch, and I was really quite unaware of the physical sensation of his entry. But all of a sudden, he was there. Slightly blue. Big. Definitely a boy. They laid him on my belly, and I pulled him up to me. He was very, very slippery. He looks like Malindi, I thought. When the doctor took him back and handed him across to a nurse, I told him to be careful, for heaven's sake, because he was so slick. The doctor said he hadn't dropped one yet. Very funny.

And now, eleven days later, he's here like he never wasn't, smelling of women's perfume from the ladies who fawn over him. He's sweet, with a furrowed brow and wonderful peering eyes that take it all in. The third child is a shadow of the first and second. His individuality is yet, for me, to be identified. He sleeps well through the night, but is inconsistent during the day. Sometimes, quite honestly, I forget that he's here, and a part of my brain is startled to come across a tiny baby in the middle of the family room, where I left him, asleep on a blanket. Or I'll come into my bedroom to get something and catch a glimpse of something on the bed out of the corner of my eye. My God: a baby!

And what a baby. Welcome to the world, Finn Thomas.

FATHER'S DAY

It was late, too late for two little girls to be bouncing off the walls. We were back from a dinner at relatives' and, while little Finn had allowed sleep to claim him, Malindi and Kenya were way too wired to contemplate such an inoperative activity. Not while there were still beds to be leaped upon, cups of water to be consumed, hamsters to be misplaced behind dressers.

A protracted session of bedroom gymnastics had not been in the plans as we'd sped across the top of the city, their father and I in the front seat, comparing plans on how to spend the evening after our sleepy offspring settled peacefully into bed: maybe watching a videotaped *West Wing*; maybe kicking back on the front porch and talking about the trouble the neighbours were having growing a lawn.

But as we reached our destination and discovered our daughters' feral state, we had no choice but to watch our free time slip rapidly into the ether — along with our dwindling hope that they were even going to fall asleep before us.

It was driving me crazy.

But Adam was philosophically idling.

And where I cursed the fading potential of our evening, he spread himself out on the lower bunk and let it — along with his giggling girls — wash over him. They were all three of them in their glory.

In the end, I retreated to my office, happy to read e-mail and veg. Sometimes parenthood, I mused from my removed post, simply asks too much of you. I have a friend who keeps insisting that she's going to call into a parent-help hotline to ask, feverishly, "When do I get to read my book?" It makes sense to me. Because we all have books to read and baths to bake in and girlfriends to telephone. And for all the time we happily invest in our kids, I always find there's a breaking point: a wall that, when I hit it, convinces me that I need to reclaim my identity and my time. You know this place. It's when you hear yourself spitting, "Enough already!" and "You kids go to bed!" in a voice that leaves no doubt that you've turned into your mother for real.

But on this night, like many before and after it, Adam hung on till the bitter end. He indulged an extended storytime, allowed himself to be a real-life hopped-on pop and played audience to a remarkably unfunny series of knock-knock jokes. At one point, I passed by the girls' bedroom door and spied the trio singing Christmas carols from a music book. I would never have found the patience, I marvelled. But Adam, a man who loves the idea of his children almost as much as he loves his children themselves, embraced them then — as he always does — for all that they are. They're just kids, he mouthed at me, as I stood frowning in the doorway at the breathless scene of late-night silliness that was dragging on and on.

Just kids, indeed.

Happy Father's Day, Adam.

TOUGH BREAK

This past weekend, I took off for Phoenix for a little R&R with a couple of girlfriends. I took the baby, Finn, with me, but would have left him behind, too, if I could have worked out a way to start Adam lactating. I deserved this break. Really, I did. Or, at least, so went my mantra in the weeks and days leading up to my departure.

Before having kids, one's freedom to come and go at a moment's notice (or at least the illusion of this freedom) is invariably squandered. You spend way too many evenings watching *M*A*S*H* reruns, and not nearly enough time cruising the latest in techno bowling alleys and all-night lingerie shops. And you certainly don't leave the living room nearly as much as you should, considering how housebound you're soon about to become.

Knowing all that, you'd think the rare opportunity to get away from it all once the kids have become your reality would be welcomed like a Popsicle on a hot day. But I couldn't do it. I couldn't allow myself to savour the sweet conjecture of a few days of relatively child-free existence (my friends and I had booked wall-to-wall babysitters for the trip) without wrestling back the dual forces of guilt and fear.

Easiest to deal with was the guilt. The kids needed some quality time with their dad, I reasoned. And, despite the huge wet eyes that stared back at me when I rattled on about how much fun their Weekend with Daddy was going to be, I managed to keep a lid on this stuff. Mostly. Mind you, there were some middle-of-the-night inner dialogues with voices that loudly reprimanded me for so capriciously abandoning my maternal duties that it was all I could do not to ring up the travel agent the next morning and lay waste to the whole crazy notion.

But fear, well, fear was another story. Leaving two children on the ground to climb aboard a hulking hunk of metal that would, in theory, suspend me in mid-air for more than four hours for the purposes of something as selfish as a gossipfest in the desert seemed foolhardy in the extreme. And if I thought myself a white-knuckled flyer before I had kids, well, I was about to discover the full extent of that whiteness. So I wrote the girls "goodbye" letters, and coached them on an assortment of wise lessons (Chew with your mouth closed, No one's buying the cow if they're getting the milk for free, etc.) that I convinced myself would tide them over into adulthood should I end up a gruesome statistic somewhere over Dayton.

In the end, I didn't let my imaginings unhinge me. I boarded the airplane. I abandoned my daughters. I took the trip. And I had a ball. Under a blazing Arizona sun, the ladies and I gabbed about everything from innovations in feminine hygiene to the relative merits of lesbianism. But, inexplicably, our conversations kept returning to one subject: our children.

It's good to be home.

FANTASTIC FINN

Dear little boy,

For that's what you are: a dear little boy. An angel from heaven spun from gold. I watch your sleeping self, outgrowing your crib, your violent tangle of yellow hair dominating the pillow. I think how peaceful you look. And how another day has drawn to a close. And as much as I treasure the silence at last, a part of me wishes your energy was still with us, bursting through bathroom doors, yanking open the fridge, turning off every light switch within (assisted) reach, spilling bowls of chili and overturning cups of grape juice.

Dear child number three, you have thrown back the doors of my experience. You have shown me how wild life can be. How loud. How joyous. From that first resisted journey into a clean morning diaper to our bedtime ritual of books on the rocker (you leaning against me with all of your weight), life has truly become an adventure.

I can see you learning now. Words. Instructions. How pleasurable it is to be along for the ride. I love watching you delight in my delight when you show off some of your talents. Like popping your pacifier out of your mouth to enunciate the "moo" of the cow in *Goodnight Moon.* Or to tell me what a duck says. Or to emerge from behind a door and announce, Hi! like some long-lost friend who loves a surprise.

You're a tough little bruiser, Finn. Your strength never ceases to amaze me. Nor your big sister Malindi, who often finds herself at the receiving end of it. But you are not a bully. Just wary. And sensitive in your treatment of the people who play roles in your life. If they're not kind to you, you won't be kind to them. Lessons like this are learned early on.

I love you, sweet Finnie McGuire. I love your fat little legs and your swaggering pot belly. I love your beautiful golden curls and your sweep of lovely eyelashes. I love how you laugh when you're tickled, and how you blurt out No! when you do something bad to pre-empt the parent you know is going to get there in the end. I love how determined you are—to put the leash on Luther, to get the top off a bottle, to reach every damn light switch in sight. I wouldn't mind it if you quit drawing on the carpet and the walls, and if you stopped sitting on the dishwasher door when I'm unloading it. But otherwise, my little guy, you can have the run of my life. And you do.

GIVING THANKS

When I was a little kid, Thanksgiving was coloured leaves and dew on the grass and dinner at bedtime because we never got the massive turkey into the oven early enough. When the feast finally materialized, my dad would struggle to liberate his legs from beneath the head of the cramped picnic table in the cottage kitchen, and get to his feet to propose a toast. The diners would hush, in deference to his projected gravitas, and I would realize, at some level, that there was a deeper meaning to this school holiday than I had previously assigned it. But then my dad would sit down, the noise would swell up again and the moment would pass.

There have been way too many Thanksgivings since then, all of them tucked into the pockets of my memory like scavenger hunt finds. I now enjoy the privilege of sitting at the adults' table instead of the makeshift arrangement with the mismatched chairs and the sense of living-room exile that was the kids' domain. But becoming a big person has had its disadvantages, too. Now I'm an unwitting member of an audience to a constant barrage of news on abductions and accidents and terrible despair. The world is suddenly filled with sadnesses more unthinkable and tragedies more arbitrary than ever would have occurred to me during those benign Thanksgiving gatherings of my childhood. And so the impulse to give thanks on this autumn day at last makes perfect sense.

I try to make my thanks both wide-ranging and specific. Of course I am thankful for my family. And for my house and my career and the various comforts of our lives. But I think it's useful to consider the exact nature of your gratitude in order that nothing — not even the way your kid mispronounces "umbrella" — gets taken for granted. For example, I am thankful for the confidences I hear my little girls exchanging in their bedroom at night. I am thankful for the sight of Finn puttering around the toy kitchen, and for the way his hair looks after a bath. I am thankful for our stroller rides to the park. And for the way my baby so fearlessly takes on every slide he encounters.

I am thankful for Kenya's wild imagination and for Malindi's extraordinarily absurd sense of humour. I am thankful for our established rituals, like the "question of the day" at bedtime, and dancing to Cat Stevens after school. I am thankful for Finnie's slippery-as-a-dolphin baby skin and for Kenya's compassion and Malindi's brown-as-coffee eyes.

I am thankful, this Thanksgiving, for the almost five years I have basked in the role of Mommy. Nothing has so changed me or so charmed me. Nothing has so poignantly reminded me to savour every sweet moment that punctuates the rushing parade of childhood. And I am thankful to have been included in the procession.

UNDER FIRE

A few months back, we had a knock on our door. It was a serious-looking young man from the Children's Aid Society, there to investigate a report that I had harmed Malindi. The CAS was following up on a conversation Kenya had had with her senior kindergarten teacher the month before, during which she had mentioned that "Mommy burned Malindi." When the teacher inquired further, she learned that I had, in search of counter space, placed Malindi down on the stove two summers ago, and, though I'd lifted her up right away, she didn't escape a minor injury from an element that had recently been on. It was scary for all of us, but Malindi was fine, and Kenya was clear on that. "Was it an accident?" the teacher had asked. "Yes," Kenya had replied.

But did that stop this odious woman from reporting us to the authorities? Not on your life.

Over the next several weeks, we were raked over a whole series of burning elements of our own. Everyone in the family was questioned, including poor Kenya, who was hauled out of class one day to talk with a strange man about what happens in her house when Mommy and Daddy get angry. They called in our pediatrician to confirm that we hadn't acted negligently in matters of our children's health in the past. And so on.

The case was dropped.

But the file was not closed, nor will it be, according to a new policy at the CAS that keeps on record allegations made against all parents, even those who have been completely exonerated. This way we'll have something to refer back to if there is a next time, the guy at the CAS explained when we phoned him for elucidation. Next time? There wasn't even a "this time."

As a mommy, I've got enough guilt in my life, thank you very much, without the CAS muscling in on this territory. Yes, I was careless. Yes, I felt miserable about causing pain to my little girl. But I've got nothing to feel ashamed about beyond that. And my little run-in with this public agency that is authorized to enforce its (arguably indiscriminate) will has just infuriated me beyond repair. Next time, if my schnauzer's incessant barking drives my neighbours round the bend, maybe they'll call the cops or the Humane Society or, really, anyone they please, and register another completely bogus accusation about me. They've seen me kicking my dog. Or they've seen me kicking my kid. And so on. Being stuck by another one of these investigative probes is not a thought I relish.

Malindi was burned, yes. But not nearly so much as I feel like I've been.

THE EXCESS OF X-MAS

Every year, we swear we're not going to do it. This Christmas, we're not going to go nuts. We listen to the advice of the level-headed folks who contain their kids' holiday bounty with some kind of clever limitation, and we enthuse over the idea of adopting such a policy ourselves. One big gift only. Drawing names. Making handmade presents. One book, one article of clothing, one toy. They all sound like such sensible plans when faced with demanding kids who are feverishly caught up in what the Saturday-morning commercials are insisting they must have.

But then Christmas Eve rolls around and I find myself — once again — afloat in a sea of presents I've amassed over the year, visions of the delight they'll bring to my kids' faces dancing in my brain. How could I resist that Barbie cat, the one that actually meows(!), for little Kenya, who's brought so much joy to our lives? Or the combination doll stroller/backpack/high chair for my poor always-in-the-middle child, Malindi? And what of Finn, the boy at the back end who's been forced to play with what must be an unhealthy overload of girls' toys since he arrived in our lives? And so on.

It's that kind of thinking that propels my purchases in the months, weeks and days leading up to Christmas. Indeed, the mad consumerist approach gathers a kind of momentum over time until, by December 24, I'm tearing through the mall, madly picking up trinkets at every turn.

To tell you the truth, in my most honest moments I must confess that I don't mind the excess that Christmas has always inspired around our house. As much as I admire the restraint other parents seem able to exercise, and even envy the lessons I imagine it must be teaching their children, I can't completely shake the feeling that Christmas should be like the party I put on every year for my kids. I love the sight of gifts cascading out from beneath the tree and stockings so full they need to be propped against the fireplace for support. I love my children's excitement as they discover the packages addressed to them. Yes, it does get crazy. Yes (Grandma), we did spend too much money. And, yes, it does eventually leave a sick feeling in the pit of my stomach as I watch them charge through the stash, barely acknowledging one gift in their pursuit of the next.

But my goodness, it is magic, that first glimpse of Christmas morning reflected in my babies' eyes. And as I take in my little sweethearts, still crazy-haired and pyjama clad, left breathless by the proof that Santa has come and gone, I console myself for all the effort and expense with which I've once again gone overboard. I will, I swear, make amends. Next year.

DESPAIR ON DISPLAY

Today, I lost it. "It" being nothing so interesting as my innocence or those last twenty pounds but, rather, my cool. We were walking from school, the four of us: Finn and Malindi in the double stroller, Kenya hanging off the side complaining that her legs were tired. In theory, we were headed to the grocery store to pick up a few things for dinner, although I must confess that the plan was a pipe dream from the start. How I imagined our particular combination of cranky after-school personalities would make its way down to the supermarket and around its aisles without incident is beyond me. But I started on the trek just the same, as hopeful as I was naive.

We made it about ten steps.

"I'm hungry," Kenya complained. I presented the piece of cheese I'd packed in anticipation of just such a grievance.

"I don't want that," she said, as if I'd just suggested she eat some of the baked-on stroller crud from within the seams of our old jalopy. I shrugged.

"And I'm thirsty," she added.

"I'll get you something to drink at the store," I offered, trying to ignore the way our perfect little outing was quickly disintegrating.

"I want something now," she whined.

I stopped the stroller. "Kenya," I said, in my most authoritative tone and fixed her with my gaze. "Watch yourself."

As if.

Whoever decided those were intimidating words for a parent to wield never tried them on an almost-six-year-old. Kenya scoffed so loudly the guys working on a house across the street looked down from their scaffolding in horror. Or so I imagined. Then it was back to the whining. "I tooooollllldd you," she said, stomping her sneakers on someone's garden-containing wall, "I'm thirsty."

That was it. I grabbed Kenya by the shoulders and started to yell. Really yell. Just how much sense the words spilling out of my mouth made is a subject best left to the crossing guard, who was following the drama from his post thirty metres away. But I know I was lobbing all kinds of ten-dollar words at the kid, words like *respect* and *attitude* and possibly even *verisimilitude.* I think I even told my daughter that "one day" she would grasp how hard it was to be a mommy, and only then would she finally realize all that I do for her and her brother and sister — and maybe then she would understand.

When that was done, I turned her around and — yup, you guessed it — swatted her bottom. Right there, I did, on the side of the road, in the company of kids on scooters and moms in minivans and everything. It was a symbolic gesture, I told myself, as I packed up and hauled my brood of children across the street in pursuit of home. Besides, Kenya was way, way out of line, and a perfunctory whack on the posterior was just the ticket.

But if my child learned a lesson from this unfortunate spectacle, I learned one too. I now know what's worse than cracking up in front of your kid: doing it with an audience.

Finn Flies Away

Today, my last little birdie flew from my nest. Nobody's going away to college here — just to the babysitter's, up the street and around the corner: a million miles away from home. Finn is nine months old. He's been outside of me as long as he was in. And now, he's taken flight across the next divide. And I am left here, third time abandoned, astonished at how the pain still pricks my mommy-bird heart.

Mine is not a novel experience. Every working mother knows the guilt, the worry, the sadness that makes the trip into the office with her after she drops her child at the daycare. I remember leaving Kenya with her first out-of-house babysitter when she was about eight months old. I limped down the walkway and back into the car, where I let it all wash over me and sobbed for ten minutes before I could even start the engine. Kenya was, of course, fine with the experience. Delighted, even, to be out of her usual surroundings, to have different toys and a different dog to play with. Completely oblivious, she was, to the wrenching torment a mommy endures when she first relinquishes her baby to another woman's care. It's like giving over your kidneys to a stranger and saying, "Here: look after these for a few hours."

I've been lucky, I suppose. Finn has spent a good chunk of his first year under his own roof. Although a nanny watched him for a couple of hours a day while I bustled upstairs to read e-mail and pretend to work, he always had the sense that Mommy wasn't far away.

And I would appear, from time to time, to unshackle a breast from my nursing bra for him, and then fade upstairs again after both of us had burped. It was, I would think as I settled back into my chair, the best of both worlds. But as I sit here at my desk today, too utterly divided to even consider work, I wonder if I haven't let the better of the worlds slip away.

I think about his face, crowned with strawberry-gold threads. I think about his eyes, and those deliciously long lashes that women will coo over all of his life. I think about his fat little hands, and his sweet, birthmark-stained bum. I wonder if he's confused about his new arrangement, if he's waiting for me to emerge from around every corner. And I wonder if he's sad that I don't.

But of course I will. And when I do (screeching to an unseemly halt in front of Rita's house and rapping my knuckles a bit too sharply on her screen door), it's all I can do not to push my way into her long hallway and snatch the little dumpling from this other woman's lap. But I sit patiently by, and listen to her tales of what a good boy Finn has been as she puts on his socks and folds his arms into his jacket. And then, at long last, my sweet fledgling is handed back to me. I wrap my wings around him and take him home.

THE BURDEN OF BERMUDA

It's not that I'm asking anyone to feel sorry for me. I am, after all, fresh off the plane from a two-week sojourn on the sunny, pink-hued shores of Bermuda. But there's something about taking a holiday with the family that leaves one wanting, er, a holiday without the family.

On the face of it, a vacation with the kids seems a lovely idea. Yes, you're all of you asked to spend an awfully long time in each other's company, but much of that is on the beach or at the swim-up bar of a hotel. Got to be better than muggy, smoggy, unswimmable Toronto, right? Not necessarily.

We were staying at Adam's brother's place, house-sitting while he and his family took off for Italy. That meant free accommodation (except for a few Canadian prezzies and a gift certificate for the toniest restaurant on the island). It also meant that Adam entered into a fifteen-day agitation over the possibility that we might render some irreparable damage to his brother's things. The rules he laid down were cruel and unusual. For one, none of us was allowed to eat indoors lest an errant crumb attract the attention of a nasty Bermudian cockroach. We routinely had to strip out of bathing suits on the front porch and endure a sand inspection before Daddy would grant entry inside. And when three-year-old Malindi had an accident on the couch on the second day, I thought the rest of us were going to have to check in at the Southampton Princess.

But it was more than Adam's ravings. Someone else's country, someone else's house (especially one filled with precious tchotchkes) is simply not the place for a trio of energetic, curious youngsters. At one point early on, I found myself harking back to a disastrous trip we had taken to Costa Rica with one-year-old Kenya. New parents, we were determined to keep up the jet-setting lifestyle. "Just strap the kid on and go" was our motto, and it lasted about as long as the drive to the airport. Kenya then was exactly the same age Finn is now, and we would have done ourselves a great service to recall the bitter vow we made at the time never to put ourselves through such torment again.

Despite fastidious efforts that included stashing all the fireplace utensils in a spare bedroom, and putting the hurricane lamps so far out of sight that we forgot to ever return them, we were no match for a baby who took his first steps while away. Finn has a special love for electronic devices, and took particular interest in the bedside clock radio, the telephone and the collection of hierarchically arranged remote controls. And so when he, on the second-last day of our holiday, disposed of my brother-in-law's bedroom TV remote, none of us should have been surprised. We turned the place upside down, but it was no use. So the last day found us gathered around the dining room table we had worked so hard to keep free of wet glass-bottom rings, scrawling out a cheery note to our hosts thanking them for their hospitality — and explaining that at least one of the wonderful conveniences of their lives was no longer. Then we skulked away from our vacation, six bags of luggage and three kids in tow, bound for the luxurious respite of our smoggy, muggy and comparatively less stressful lives in Toronto.

Clothes Comfort

I remember the red sleeper with the man fishing from the moon on it that baby Kenya wore her first winter. I remember the fleecy playsuit with the hood that we tucked little Malindi into when it got so cool that summer evening. I remember the linen outfit with the pearl domes that I bought for my unborn Finn, the day the ultrasound had revealed he was a boy.

They're just clothes, my mother will exclaim, when she sees me getting weepy in the basement the day I finally get around to sorting through everything none of my babies will ever wear again. But they're more than that. They're memories, as palpable as cotton between your fingers. Each recalls a tale of a little person at an earlier stage of her evolution; a picture in time of a new family, a new experience, a new life. Back when "Mom" was still "Mommy." When a maternal kiss healed all boo-boos. Before best-friend anxiety or Britney Spears or bellybutton-baring shirts. Along with baby vitamins and spit-up, each of these little garments is stained with nostalgia.

I remember buying Kenya that man-in-the-moon sleeper from a consignment store when she was just a few weeks old. I can still recall the delight I took in the littleness of the garment, and the way my heart sang with the knowledge that I finally had a sweet baby of my own to play dress-up with. I remember Malindi's playsuit arriving, a gift from friends, and how I couldn't wait for an evening cool enough to slip my second sweet babe into it. And I remember the fateful trip to Gymboree, fresh from the ultrasound where the unsettling news that I was having a boy this time had sent me into a tailspin. I was intent on finding something cute for this tiny alien, to ease the jolt. I stared at that petite linen outfit for five months before Finn's arrival put the last niggling doubts to rest.

And now here I sit in the basement, faced with the prospect of having to cast all of these remembrances aside. And I can't pretend it's not breaking my heart to realize there's no one left to wear that awful, pilly Mulan nightgown. Or the faux velvet jumpsuit Kenya wore the Easter she was four months old. Or the little Chuckroast fleece suit that kept all of my babies warm their first winters on this planet.

Parting with kids' clothes — whether they're bound for consignment stores or the astonishingly small offspring of friends and relatives — is a ritual with which all mothers are painfully familiar. This is the changing of the clothing guard that's as much a part of Canada's twice-yearly weather turnabout as storm windows and firing up the furnace. The tucking away of the sweaters and mitts when late spring finally makes a commitment. The hauling out of long pants and turtlenecks when the chill returns in the fall.

But my semi-annual purge is not nearly as exhaustive as it might be. No matter how ruthless my intentions might be when I descend the basement steps, my fingers will invariably fasten onto something from within one of the legion Tupperware tubs that inhabit the landscape down there, and my eyes will mist with memory as I yank it to the surface. In no time, I'm lost in a reverie over that one-piece autumn coverup, say, or the tiny grey hooded sweatshirt that all three babies wore, or the little red bikini whose two parts I remember Malindi's round baby belly emerging between. I'll stare at the piece of cloth clutched in my hands, recalling a place in time that slipped away too soon. A new person, trying out her walking legs on a sidewalk scattered with autumn leaves. A wailing infant, whose sweet-cheeked face grows ever redder with indignation within the circle of her fleece hood. A cherubic beach baby sifting sand between her fingers. And I can't let go. So I sigh, and deposit yet another piece of carefully folded memory onto the "keep" pile, rather than onto the more sensible one that's bound for a destination outside of our increasingly crowded closets.

I even have trouble discarding outgrown footwear, although I know that no other kids — mine or other people's — will ever wear these affronts to the senses again. I've never gone ahead and gotten any of these things bronzed, and as the collection of too-small shoes gets ever bigger — in number and in size — my rationale for why I held on to them in the first place gets buried deeper in the stash. Just more stuff to cling to, I suppose, for fear that the parting might somehow cancel out the memory. Maybe I'll make a couple of shoe wall hangings for the family room.

We have a ritual in our house. A few weeks before our new baby is set to make an appearance, just as the delicious mixture of panic and excitement is starting to fill the air, Adam and I make a trip to the mall. We go in pursuit of a "coming-home outfit," something that we'll negotiate the fresh pink limbs of our little newcomer into when we're given the green light to leave the hospital. All three of my children have had outfits, with matching beanie caps and tiny undershirts. I've let them wear the clothes a few times only, and then tucked them away lest they become sullied with too many off-colour mementos of infancy. Ultimately, I've arranged each in a shadow box which I've hung on bedroom doors whence I can regularly marvel over their impossible tininess. My oldest is about to turn six. When I regard her gangly, elongating self against the doll-sized sleeper suspended at the entrance to her room, my mind simply cannot fathom that the same child inhabited both realities.

Down in the basement, I finally manage to fill two large containers with children's clothing which I ask Adam to deliver to the consignment store. I don't dare pry back the lids again, even if I think I've left the hamster in there, or second thoughts are bound to overwhelm me. Just the same, I've amassed a considerable collection of holdbacks: little jean jackets, size four suede mountain boots (into which I was able to stuff uncooperative baby feet precisely twice), great-grandma-knitted sweaters, the tiny cardigan with the elephants and lions, the Scottie-dog overalls and the baptismal baby bonnet. And I've stashed them all onto a top shelf above the dollies and the Disney beanie bags where I hope I won't have to think about them for a while. What those clothes are waiting for is beyond me. For another child, perhaps — mine or someone else's? For an inventive means of preserving and displaying them that won't overly tax my already overly taxed wallspace? Or perhaps just for another opportunity to transport me back, even as I am travelling forward, to the talcum-scented, promise-filled days and nights of my babies' beginnings.

THE NUMBERS GAME

At a certain level, I regard children as I do cardigans for sale at the mall. My impulse, when I see some lovely chenille number, is to buy a half dozen in different colours. Why not? I reason. If one of them will bring me joy, wouldn't six bring me that much more?

To decide that you're "done" having children is to slam shut a door on the shopping experience altogether. And what a great tragedy that would be. I mean, what's the point of having a Gap right in your neighbourhood if you never go in it? What's more, you get this flood of flyers every month to remind you of the store's existence — and of all the wonderful things you might find there — and all you can do is take a Midol and stay at home.

There aren't many touchier topics with a woman than whether she's going to have any more kids. Some women are definite: "I always knew I'd stop at two." Others are conflicted: "I want to but he doesn't." But most are wishy-washy, and their response exposes the massive internal struggle that — thanks to advances in modern science — can rage on in the background of women's lives until they're riding buses on seniors' fares: "We're still trying to decide."

Let's face it, if we behaved as nature had intended, we'd just keep buying up those sweaters until menopause took our credit cards away. But most of us don't have the time, the money, the house or the attention span for the kinds of families our grandparents made. And so we all have to settle on a number. One sounds perfect, but two might be better. And wouldn't three be lovely? Mind you, four is such an even sum. And so on.

Why is it so hard to draw the line? For one, it's agonizing to realize that each milestone your youngest reaches will be the last. For all time. No more little knit caps and matching booties. No more first smiles, first steps, first words. The only first on the horizon for these kids now is first base in the back of the family Caravan.

Or maybe it's because the moment you accept that you'll never have another child is the same moment you accept that, aside from the odd wedding and really wicked graduation party, the next watershed event in your life will be your death. What better way to thumb your nose at the aging process than to squeeze out another baby?

And so we put off the inevitable and hold nature at bay. "Let's just say no one's getting anything snipped yet" is our standard response to the folks who wonder if we could possibly go for another. My youngest is fifteen months, and I still trip over his damn baby swing in my office every day. Sure, I could take it down and haul it — along with the numerous car seats, bouncy chairs, Jolly Jumpers and sensory-stimulating crib mobiles — to the kids' consignment shop up the street. But I don't. I won't even throw out the leftover maternal vitamins. Instead, I join the multitude of women who tuck cute names into the attics of their brains "just in case." Who pause over the carriage of a freshly minted person and let the pangs wash over them. Who understand that baby hunger is a female epidemic.

And here I sit, with three absolutely darling sweaters in my closet — enough for even the most avaricious of clotheshorses — wondering whether I should trot down to the mall and pick myself up just one more.

FOURTH TIME'S THE CHARM

I must admit I had a feeling. Suddenly, the world was so much more pungent than before. Coffee smelled stronger. So did plastic. And everybody seemed to be cooking onions at the same time. Something was up. And, as it turned out, it was the level of pregnancy hormones in my bloodstream.

I took the test on my own, on a Saturday morning when Adam was delivering Kenya to gymnastics. Malindi and Finn and I had ventured out into the throngs of revelers gathered for a Ukrainian festival in our neighbourhood. The lady at the local drugstore raised her voice above the din to ask where my third child was, and I can't tell you how sheepish I felt putting a home pregnancy test on the counter between us as I answered. I couldn't get out the door fast enough.

And, while we're on the subject of doors, I should say that I'd never entirely shut one on the notion of having a fourth child. So passionate am I about my role as mommy, so enamoured am I with tiny babies, that declaring that I would never have another was simply too painful to bear. And yet, I'd spent the fifteen months since Finn was born working to convince my soul that such thoughts were pure fantasy for an already overburdened working mom of three. I only realized how successfully I'd persuaded myself when I misinterpreted the results of the pregnancy test. Hovering over the plastic stick balanced on the side of the tub, I sighed with profound relief when a single blue line appeared. Then, to my horror, a second line emerged — and my heart sank. Four kids. I was going to be mother to a euchre party.

Later that day, against the bustling backdrop of the festival, I told the father-to-be the news. This way, I'd figured, Adam's screams of anguish would be muffled by the cries coming from the Berry Go Round. But his first instinct, bless his heart, was to be delighted. Adam loves new babies as much as I, and he confessed that his first blush of joy was pure reflex. Afterwards, other shades set in.

Several weeks later, we are all coming to terms with our new reality. Adam's taken an abundance of long walks and I've made a new acquaintance with the interior of the toilet bowl. When we told the kids about the new baby, Malindi was delighted because she thought this meant we could "put Finn back in," in exchange for someone who didn't pull her hair quite so much. We've even shared our news with all the relatives, including the grandmothers, who believe it's foolhardy to do anything more than replace yourself on this earth. Clearly, we're working with a different philosophy.

All that remains now? To await the arrival of our next family member, a new little person whose presence initially shocked the pants off me, but with whom I have already fallen in love.

THE DISTINCTION OF BOYS

I've always been amused at the names given to hurricanes: harmless-sounding tags, like Gretchen, and José, that don't quite jibe with the destruction they wreak. I'd like to submit a more applicable handle for the next one. Finn.

My son is a force of nature. Indeed, he's right up there on the Beaufort scale. A twelve, at least.

Oh, we'd been warned what it would be like to have a boy. And with two girls already in play, we were blessedly aware of the male-female distinction, thanks particularly to testosterone exposure during park excursions. The little boys would be the madly rushing creatures: throwing sand, stealing pails, shoving each other down the slides. The little girls, meanwhile, would be more reserved, playing quietly under oak trees, sharing their Goldfish crackers, helping elderly ladies to the park bench. Mind you, it's possible that bitter experience has caused me to redraft the whole affair slightly in my memory. But certainly the nuances between the sexes were not lost on me before I became a keeper of both.

And then I had myself a boy.

The moment Finn was mobile, he headed straight for our CD rack, and proceeded to categorically remove every case, open it and break the shiny silver disk inside. When he was about a year, he learned how to open the fridge. He goes there regularly now, to try a taste of all the beverages lined up in the door, to fling open yogourt containers across the floor and to catapult eggs, one by one, from their nifty cardboard carton. Once, he broke a beer bottle, showering glass shards across the kitchen floor. I tried to soften the incident with his fuming father by casting it as his son's first exposure to a cold brew, but Adam was unimpressed.

And God help us if we had any intentions of preserving the electronic gadgetry in our household. From eight months, Finn could unhitch the back panel of the remote control and remove the batteries, a prize for his efforts which he would then jam in his mouth and happily suck. Cellphones are also favourites, and he's proven it by dropping two of them into the bathtub.

Mind you, dropping is a specialty for this boy. In addition to unloading food from his high-chair tray (always accompanied by an innocent "uh-oh"), Finn relinquishes all manner of matter down the open heating vents throughout the house (I keep saying we've got to get the covers replaced). Among other things, he's committed toys, chalk, toothbrushes, Barbies and keys to that underground abyss.

Don't get me wrong. I wouldn't trade my little cyclone for the world. He's a lovely lad. He's curious, funny, charming with the ladies and easygoing as all get out. And this kid's got spunk. If he spies something he wants, even if it's that cup of coffee you've put on the highest shelf to dodge his reach, you'd better be prepared to fight his advances on it to the end.

And it's the celebration of that dogged determination with which his daddy and I comfort each other — nightly — as we recount the calamities of the day. I also encourage him to join me in the mantra I recently adopted to endure the wonderful peculiarities of being parent to a son: "This too shall pass."

RUSH HOUR

Mornings around our house last all day. Or at least that's how it seems, when you're in the midst of one of them.

Take this morning, for example, a typical Monday during which various children are expected to return to various institutions of education and childcare. Adam typically has to rush off early on the first day of the week, and therefore is blissfully exempt from our delirious scramble to get up and out of the house.

I always start with myself. It's like the thoughtful advice the folks on the airlines give, about availing yourself of the oxygen mask before tending to your kid. Thanks to my pregnant state, my day generally begins with a trip to the bathroom for a solid bout of dry heaves. Then I clean myself up, slip into whatever still fits and head for the girls' bedroom.

I consider myself extraordinarily blessed to have children who enjoy their sleep. It's wonderful on the weekend not to be swarmed by little people demanding cinnamon toast just as I'm settling into the next in my series of Brad Pitt dreams. But on the weekdays, administering to reluctant-to-rouse children is hell on wheels.

This time, I had cleverly slipped into Kenya and Malindi's room before my own ablutions, to open the shutters and turn on the lights. It would be an early warning knell, I reasoned. By the time I reached them, they would be alert and entirely receptive to facing the day. No such luck. The girls were still deeply asleep when I alighted on the edge of the bed and trilled that it was "time to get up." I ended up having to dress them both in their sleep, an exercise which included such rewards as vitriol, condemnation and a couple of kicks to the gut.

I plowed forward just the same, even attempting to brush their teeth and insisting on brushing Kenya's hair (I would have been inviting a twenty-minute delay — minimum — if I had even attempted Malindi's). Then I left them — still grumbling — in front of cartoons in my room, and ventured in to greet a burbling Finn, who took pity on me and let me change his diaper and dress him with minimal fuss.

Downstairs, I discovered the remnants of last night's dinner still strewn across the kitchen. Nonplussed, I brushed the dried turkey and tomato bits off the table and dropped bowls of oatmeal and plates of pancakes in their place. As the kids ate, swallowing mouthfuls between complaints about the choice of breakfast offerings, I squeezed their feet into footwear, packed knapsacks full of morning snacks and less-than-complete homework, retrieved the package of diapers from the upstairs hall that I needed to deliver to Finn's babysitter and herded the crew out to the van. It was, of course, parked a block up the street. By the time we were all seatbelted in, the school bell had long since gone off.

After depositing Kenya in the schoolyard and urging her to rush to her classroom lest we get another "late" strike against our good name, we slid in just under the bell at Malindi's nursery school, three-and-a-half blocks away. Then it was on to Finn's babysitter. I brought him up to her door, and then ran back to the van to retrieve the forgotten diapers. We parted with a snotty kiss goodbye and, at last, the morning ritual was over. And not a moment too soon.

REVELATIONS

The hardest part of being pregnant for a fourth time, as it turns out, isn't the heartburn. It isn't the waddle or the way my pelvis feels like it's been split up the middle. And it isn't even the wardrobe, though I can pretty much assure you that all items of elasticized clothing will be discarded from my collection the moment I can contemplate a waistband again. No, the hardest part of being pregnant for a fourth time is the telling. The witness I must regularly bear to a dawning revelation on people's faces when, as I round the corner into the sixth month, they realize my burgeoning secret. *Surely she's not pregnant again?* You betcha.

The schoolyard moms are the worst. Most of us are mere acquaintances, nodding perfunctory greetings across the hoods of our strollers as we negotiate a chunk of pavement outside the side doors in anticipation of ringing bells. But there are definite maternal cliques, groups of women who while the wait away with little knots of gossip. And their expressions, as they process the information with which my swelling self, shambling into view, has confronted them, is priceless. You can almost hear the inner monologue as it spins out of their brains: "Hey, is she...? Naw, she couldn't be, she already has three kids, for Pete's sake! But it sure looks like it... Good lord, I have to ask Lillian..."

And the reactions I've enjoyed from the people with whom I've come clean from the get-go haven't been much better. They assume it was a big fat mistake. And although they're right, something in me bristles at the speculation that a decent woman in this day and age would never choose a houseful of children unless she's some religious loony or otherwise soft in the head. So they get this unfortunate look of combined shock, pity and disgust on their faces that I want to slap off.

Even family members — particularly family members, come to think of it — have received my happy news tepidly. And I suppose I've approached the announcement expecting nothing less. Or more, as the case may be. I told my parents and brother about our little development in a cowardly e-mail which included numerous displays of self-flagellation. A far cry from that jubilant pronouncement about my first glowing introduction to maternity. When we told my nana at Thanksgiving dinner, she responded with utter silence. I dare say the turkey carcass that sat on the table between us provided a more gratifying response than she did. And then there was the day I planned to tell my grandmother. We were gathered in my parents' kitchen, a six-weeks-pregnant me steeling my nerves for the Big Announcement, when Grandma declared out of the blue that she hoped I was scheduling a tubal ligation because the last thing we needed was one more child. Needless to say, I chickened out. My mother dropped the bomb on my behalf later, and I eventually found the courage to strike up a relationship with the old woman again.

Let's face it, once you've brought a pair of children into this world, the unspoken assumption is that you're done, and anything more would either be a terrible blunder or such a reckless display of poor judgement that an entirely uncensored response would be the only appropriate one. While first and second pregnancies are things of unabashed joy, inflated affirmations of hope and truth to be trumpeted to the world, subsequent gestational forays are different matters. These are shameful developments to be hidden under parkas and bad lighting. Most folks, it seems, can't bear to face the reality of other people's brazen fertility.

But what's done is done. So I've taken to flaunting my astonishingly — and increasingly — large person in others' midsts. Now I delight in watching the raised eyebrows and hearing the sharp intakes of breath as I shrug off my coat. Yes, I am, I say with my eyes, just daring them to respond with anything less than pure elation. Generally, it works. They take the bait and applaud my apparent courage. Better you than me, they fawn, from within my enormous shadow. And I smile, and rub a hand across my expansive belly. At least we can agree on something.

END OF THE INNOCENCE

"S-E-X," said my five-year-old, as she hunched over a piece of paper at the dining room table, pencil gripped in hand. In the living room, struggling to decipher the code on our new digital TV system, I about dropped my spleen.

"What was that, Kenya?" I sang out cheerily, sidling over to her side with a silly grin pasted on my mug.

"S-E-X," she repeated, adding the final touches to the word that I discovered to be, indeed, scrawled onto the sheet in front of her. "Ashmir made her own little book, and put that on the cover. I want to, too."

"Oh," I chirped, and then adopted my very best dumbspeak-for-kids voice: "And what does that spell?"

"Sex," she said, like I was the dummy.

"Mmmm-hmmm," I said, leaning my elbows onto the table in the event that my legs gave way. "And what does that mean?"

"I think it means 'neat,'" Kenya said, and I finally remembered to breathe. That will do, for now. But the messy business of adult recreational activities — and all of the attendant questions that go with them — can only be kept at bay for so much longer.

It's not that I'm scared of venturing into this territory. I've read all the articles and listened to all the latest words of wisdom on how to broach such Big Topics of Conversation. I guess I was just hoping not to have to do any broaching for, oh, another fifteen or twenty years, give or take. Because, at the end of the day, the hardest thing about having children is letting them ever be anything but. It's why I don't mind that my three-year-old still wanders through life with a pacifier stuck in her gob. It's why I like that my five-year-old isn't embarrassed to hold my hand or kiss me goodbye in front of her friends. And why I (secretly) treasure the idea that I still have two kids in diapers.

It's sick, I know. But I'll get mine. The day of reckoning is fast approaching. Indeed, some of the adult intrigue I've worked so assiduously to conceal has already leaked out. Kenya is aware that boys sometimes chase girls around the schoolyard. She knows who Britney Spears is, and she even knows about French kissing (but she's in French immersion, so I framed this one as a cultural lesson).

With each revelation, a little piece of me grieves for the loss of childhood innocence, inevitable as it may be. Yes, another, more responsible and realistic part of me (possibly my liver), acknowledges the transition as a healthy part of the journey to adulthood. But that one makes me gag. Sigh. It's so much easier to program a digital TV.

THE MATERNAL SECRETARY

The thing about being a parent is that so much more is expected of you than they let on in the guide books. Sure, they're up front about the love and care for thing. About the wiping snotty noses and sloppy bums thing. Even about the sleepless nights thing. But nobody ever says boo about how mothers are also expected to act as personal secretaries to their pint-sized bosses, and just how demanding that job will be. How it falls to Mommy to contain in her already overloaded brain all manner of administrative minutiae, including which library books are due back at which library when, what day of the week her child has pledged to furnish the class with thirty-four Rice Krispie squares, and what footwear is required in accordance with the planned activities of a child's afternoon.

At this point in my life, only one of my children is in school, which means that keeping track of homework assignments, field trips, choir practices, and show and tells is not as onerous a task as it might — and will — be. But Malindi attends nursery school three mornings a week, and Finn is with a babysitter during those same periods. At every turn, there are instructions and expectations.

Fortunately, Malindi's requirements are few. The nursery school never ventures outside the facility's doors, so there's no need to include a change of shoes or even particularly warm outerwear. On top of that, snacks are provided and the nursery school students don't engage in the ritual of either showing or telling. As for Finn, I need only remember to dress him in a snowsuit on Mondays and Fridays, because that's when his sitter needs to walk several blocks to pick up another charge down the street. And I've got to take care not to put him in his thick socks on those days, because they're too bulky to cram into his snow boots. I also need to pack a snack and juice, and to remember to use the cups with the little rubber valves and not the ones with the straws and spouts since the latter are more likely to explode when you open them. If Rita asks for diapers one day, or tells me she's almost out of wipes, I need to make a mental note to pack them up in his bag the next time we go.

But Kenya is the real work. Just in grade one, she's providing us with our first real taste of juvenile bureaucratic routine. And let me tell you, we're struggling. In addition to the standard professional development and stat holidays, we're having to remember that every day five is library day, that music and phys ed alternate, that the last Friday of every month is pizza day. We need to pack her up with her borrow-a-books on Monday, to return her final spelling test booklet — signed — on Thursday and to hand in her book report package the first of every month. Fridays are practice spelling tests; Tuesdays are finals. On Tuesday lunch, she has French choir practice; English choir is a half hour before school starts on Wednesdays. If they send work home in the big manila envelope, we must take back said envelope the following day. We need to return field trip permission forms and pizza money and our order sheets for school photos sometime before the kid graduates to the next grade.

In the fall, Kenya brought home one of those bulky coupon booklets — the school's latest fund-raising ploy — and a form requesting thirty-two dollars for its purchase. We immediately lost the booklet. But I'm happy to report that I did remember to send Kenya in with a cheque paying for it. Such are the slender, twisted victories of playing personal secretary to the bustling schedule of a child.

FIRST GRADE

In way too few days and hours and minutes, my eldest child will be going off to grade one. Marching down the street, through the schoolyard and into the rest of her life.

After two years in the glorified nursery school that is kindergarten, during which time she was still mine for half a day, she is my baby no longer. My sweet, sensitive little Kenya — who sleeps with a stuffed hippo and cries if she thinks you're laughing at her — is about to be introduced to the serious business of the school system. To become flotsam on the vast ocean of necessary education.

It's been more than ten years since I stepped off my own school-steered raft. But I never stopped feeling under the influence of the academic tides. At last, the urge to buy a new package of coloured pencils that grips me every Labour Day will be validated through the experience of my daughter. Any excuse to legitimize a trip to the mall.

And so on some level I look forward to this watershed. Having Kenya in school full-time also means no more child care for one quarter of my children. There's a certain measure of satisfaction in that. And I can't wait to relearn all the stuff the years and pregnancies and nighttime feedings have crowded out of my brain. French verb conjugations, periodic elements, common denominators: bring it all on. I envision cozy scenes around the dining room table, Kenya and I hunched over her homework, giggling like schoolgirls, possibly wearing matching kilts. That the reality will probably more closely resemble a WWE mother-daughter matchup is something I try not to dwell on.

Mostly, though, the big day fills me with more melancholy than it does joy. When I hark back to the tiny creature who graced us first with twitching baby smiles and then full belly laughs, who lay between us in bed like a princess and whose best views of the world were from her stroller, I can't believe how far we've come. Imagine: that same giddy toddler whose little white bum used to charge through the hallway when we chased her after a bath now closes the washroom door behind her and is self-conscious about calling me "Mommy" in front of her friends. She's embarrassed that her bike still has training wheels, and she scours her closet every morning for "something pretty."

And on top of it all, she is now a student, bound for years and years and years of education, including the kind that comes from being overlooked for the birthday party invitations handed out at recess, playing spin the bottle in the schoolyard fort and getting her period through her pants in geography class. That the world will be kind to my sweet sailor as she navigates her scholarly path is my fiercest wish.

WEANING FINN

Five nights ago, I fed my baby from my breast for the last time. It was uneventful enough, unaware as we both were that it was at all a significant occasion. The next night, I wouldn't nurse him at all.

I've been thinking about weaning Finn for the last several months. I don't feed him much anymore: just at bedtime and then once or twice when he wakes in the night. But it's those night wakings that are the buggers, and I knew in my gut that cold turkey from the breast (to be distinguished from cold breast from the turkey) was probably the best solution.

After all, one look at my Finnie, and it's clear this guy does not want for food. His journeys to my milk ducts long ago made the transition from the pursuit of nourishment to the pursuit of comfort alone. Not that there's anything wrong with that. Except when it keeps me from my slumber.

Our nighttime ritual — on the first night I would not breastfeed my baby — began as it had every night for the sixteen months since baby Finn had been in our lives. There was the transformation from lollipop-sticky toddler into scrubbed-face, pyjama-clad sleepyhead. There were the usual wrestles to get teeth brushed, and to keep Finn from attacking his middle sister as she sat on the toilet. Then there was the procession of pre-settle antics that include: running around the second floor like a banshee, jumping on Mommy and Daddy's bed until one kid lands on the body part of another kid, pulling the duvet off the bed and making like a giant, three-headed monster who constantly alarms Mommy with its proximity to the top of the stairs.

After that, it was book time, which saw Daddy sprawled on Kenya and Malindi's bed, buffeted by two little girls. Finnie, meanwhile, wandered in and out of the scene, pulling clothes out of drawers, climbing the highest point in the room, and tormenting the cats, who had sought refuge in the closet.

On other nights, I would arrive at a certain point to scoop the little fellow up and retreat with him to the relative solitude of my bedroom. We would flick off the light and arrange ourselves on the bed, me sitting cross-legged, baby Finn cradled in my lap. Sometimes I would flick the TV on and meander through the channels. Sometimes I would just gaze at the sweet suckling face, so earnestly indulging in its evening meal. This was our special time, and I've treasured it from that very first day that my new baby's arrival from the hospital gave him and me an excuse to separate ourselves from the hullabaloo of big-kid bedtime.

But on this night, we didn't go into my bedroom at all. I just deposited little Finn in his crib. I pulled up his quilt, and kissed his fat cheek. And then I shut the door.

I left his room determined to return and reverse my decision at the slightest protest. If my little guy seemed overly insistent or desperately sad, I would postpone the whole thing. After all, the decision not to nurse on this night had been a spontaneous one. And I was never entirely committed to the idea. But my sweet baby slipped off to sleep without the benefit of my special maternal comfort, and didn't seem to miss it at all. When he woke up crying, I went in and sat with him on my lap, gliding in the darkness in our rocking chair. I put him back down without a fight.

That my little boy has so effortlessly mastered this passage into the next phase of his youth fills me with a whole tangle of emotions. I'm delighted he's so sanguine about pulling off one of life's first challenges. But my God, when I think on this milestone too long, my chest aches — and in a place well behind the source of milk.

TO KENYA, AT AGE SIX

Dear sweet little Kenya Lee,

It is months past your sixth birthday, but I have been too overwhelmed — both with the business of daily life, and with the prospect of accurately capturing my oldest child six years into the adventure — to write.

You, my lovely girl, are a piece of work. A work in progress, actually, often with all the gears and mechanics exposed (to my great delight). Every day, I see more evidence of the person you are to become emerging from the person you are like the pages of a mystery.

My omniscient child, nothing gets past you. Still, you are a bundle of contradictions. You are sensitive and sweet — and whiny and stubborn. You appreciate everything, and nothing at all. You are as demanding as a newborn; but often so independent my heart aches with a need to be needed.

Over the heads of your siblings, I see you watching me. Taking it in. Learning what it is to be a mother, a wife, a woman. You judge me, and ask questions. You want to know why I'm punishing Malindi. Why Finn is crying. I saw you, you say, after witnessing a fight I have with your father. And I am caught once again in your headlights. But I ultimately welcome the challenge. I will teach you, my love. And mistakes are part of the learning.

Tonight, as I painstakingly crammed Malindi into her favourite "feet pyjamas," I let my mind travel back to the days when you wore this pale yellow delicacy. I can remember how round your cheeks were. And how your eyes became slits when you beamed us a smile. I remember episodes, like the time you bit Brianna, and the route through the schoolyard we used to take home from Rita's. I remember feeling proud of how sensible and restrained you were. Feeling scared during your terrors at night. Feeling huge with the motherhood of you.

But the memories are all intellectual. Everything tactile has gone, swept away on the push of time. I peer into photographs like they're my salvation, hoping to unearth something more than just the scrap of a plot from the movie of your early life. But alas. The tangible recollections are all victims of progress.

So I turn my gaze on you now, ever hopeful of imprints of permanence. Those green eyes that sparkle with knowing mischief, then darken under the furrow of an exaggerated brow. That lovely smattering of freckles on that textbook-perfect nose. Those lengthening limbs, always extending their reach away from babyhood and towards adolescence.

These are my touchstones. My yardstick against which I measure my role as a mother. Before there was you, Kenya, there was only me. You made me us.

I love you, little girl. Even after the seventh nighttime visit from you, this one announcing that your nose is stuffed up (to follow on from a spectrum of complaints about sore toes and spidery hair and a mysteriously unquenchable bedtime thirst). I love you in the morning, when I gather your pyjamaed body up onto my lap and relish the privilege of still doing so. I love you at lunch, when I catch sight of your orange ski jacket, and watch your serious little face seeking me out across the crowds (*Je vois ma maman*, you'll announce to the teacher, and then gallop towards me). I love you after school, when you whine about wanting a friend to come over. I love you with your sister, a moment without strife when the pair of you play cars or dolls together, and I let my mind yawn forwards to the adult versions of you. I love you with your brother, more protective and adoring than I ever could have hoped for in a big sister. And I love you when your eyes catch mine, and you see that I'm exhausted. Or concerned. Or just in love with the idea of being your mother. And something in the way you look at me lets me know that you appreciate it. Those are the moments, my love. Those are the ones that are burned on my brain.

COMING TO TERM

Part of me, nine months into the mission, still cannot believe that I'm going to have another baby. That I'm going to have my fourth baby, for heaven's sake. That I'm going to go through labour and delivery and breastfeeding and sleepless nights...again. That I'm going to bear witness to a new human being's transitions from sitting up to crawling to walking...again. It almost seems surreal to imagine that I'm going to travel through these passages once more — and in the company of a new little stranger who is still part of my body.

I remember way back when I had Kenya, six-and-a-half amazing years ago, wondering how my life would change once I added this new little person to it. Of course there was no way to predict. She came along and she threw my daily — and nightly — existence on its backside. But I managed. I worked around her, both figuratively and literally. Her naptimes were put to productive use. Sometimes a mother's helper took her for walks around the block. And when she was old enough, I shipped her off to a grandmotherly woman up the street who cared for her three half-days a week. The guilt over her exile was considerable, but my options were limited and I gradually came to accept that.

Then, two-and-a-half years later, Kenya's sister came along. Malindi's arrival really threw me for a loop, because I suddenly had two people's schedules to fit around my own. The arrangement was highly unpredictable and set me up for a lot of stressful afternoons.

Eventually, I retrieved my firstborn from her up-the-street sitter and invited a friend of mine into the house, along with her little girl, to look after Kenya and to act as a fallback when baby Malindi was screaming at times that were inconvenient with my work schedule.

Then, before you could say "have you considered birth control?" I was pregnant with number three. How the heck I was ever going to wedge this person into my routine was beyond me. Initially, I continued to rely on the help of my in-house babysitter pal, who was so incredibly competent that she managed her own two (she'd given birth in the meantime) and my three from the basement of my home with nary a hiccup. But then it all became too much, and I went through a string of less-than-caring caregivers before sending Malindi to nursery school and Finn to Kenya's former up-the-street sitter three mornings a week. Kenya, mercifully, had graduated to grade one (and full-time school) by this point.

And now here I sit, huge with number four, having at last discovered a work-and-childcare plan that makes sense with my three kids, wondering once again how I'm going to make all the pieces fall into place. In a perfect world, I would have a coach house, just this side of an in-ground pool, that would be home to my astonishing brood of offspring. They would thrive there under the capable custody of various nannies whose imaginative approach to childcare would all but relieve my guilt for not spending every minute of the day in their company.

Sigh.

More likely: I'll sign on some half-baked and transitory babysitter to look after the two little ones while the two bigger ones are in school (Malindi starts half-days this fall), and I'll wince in pain from my upstairs office at each little wail to which I'm not attending, occasionally dissolving into weeping despair on my keyboard wrist rest.

PLASTIC PROPRIETY

I think it was the guy in *The Graduate* who made a pronouncement, way back in the 1960s, that plastics was the business to get into. No kidding.

My life, since it became seriously overrun with little kids, has become an exercise in managing small pieces of plastic. Not a day goes by when I'm not confronted with the challenge of what to do with myriad bits of colourful crap. We must have a hundred Barbie hairbrushes, dozens of tiny tubs of body glitter ferried home in one loot bag after another, a casino's worth of colourful plastic dice. The other day, Adam was pouring himself a cup of tea and was not in the least surprised when a Monopoly hotel surfed out of the kettle spout. And don't even get me started on those valuable little add-ons they include in Happy Meals.

Then there's the particular category of plastic-coated paraphernalia that I hold on to for precisely the same reason I keep a drawer of unmatched socks in my bedroom: the tiny Spirograph circles, long since separated from their siblings; the marker lids, whose thirsty companions I continue to believe might still someday appear; the numbered balls from the billiards set Kenya got for Christmas (although I believe I put the table out in the trash some months ago).

Once every few months, I feel the weight of the plastic too heavily, and commit myself to getting a handle on it. From there, it's off to Ikea and Canadian Tire, returning home with all manner of storage solutions. Like a madwoman, I whirl through the family room, dumping one toy bin after another onto the floor. The children are forbidden from entering the playroom during this time: this work, after all, is not kid stuff.

Thus confronted with the full bounty of my family's plastic stash, I set about introducing order. The first step in the conquest is to divide the mess into categories. There's the animal section, into which I herd an amazing number of tiny plastic rabbits, sheep, elephants and turtles. There's the transportation section, for plastic cars, motorbikes, fire trucks and boats. I start an "accessories" category, to house Barbie's tiny pumps, Madeline's belts and Polly Pocket's hand mirrors. I even designate one plastic tub for "balls" and take great delight in tossing dozens of rubber orbs into it. Occasionally, I am faced with great dilemmas, like whether to put Finn's plastic dress-up shoes with the "girl make-believe" stuff or in the "boy imaginative play" bin. And I wrestle constantly with miscellany whose provenance I am unable to determine accurately. In the end, I assign one large tub "sundry" and vow to return to it later.

At the end of it all, I am spent. The ridiculously intricate Kinder Egg booty has all been sorted, the checker disks (we're short two red and one black, but I'm hopeful) have been locked in the "games" box and the Mr. Potato Head ears have been tucked into the rear ends of their hosts. The McDonald's toys have been sorted into two piles: trash and collectibles. And every last plastic fried egg, Tinker Toy, Mulan figurine and Playmobil coffee mug has been assigned a home.

I take a deep breath, filled with the sweetness of order and reason. And then I holler to Adam, "Release the hounds!" The kids, no doubt smelling the promise of freshly systematized plastic, rush in.

WELCOME, KAIKOURA

As much in a blink of an eye as in the nine months leading up to it, I have become a mother to four children. Mind you, I had three already in the pot: it was just a matter of adding the sugar. The dessert. And that is how we think of Kaikoura Grace. She is our final, sweet helping of child.

She arrived two days late, finding me just on the edge of a scream of overcooked frustration. I was vast and wildly uncomfortable. The heartburn had reached epic proportions. My sleep was repeatedly broken by creaking trips on aching legs to the bathroom. And my wild imaginings about what life with a quartet of children six and under was going to be like were ruling my every waking thought.

I'd had more than a week of false labour (including one early-morning call to my parents to get their butts in gear before I gave birth in the living room) when we went out for dinner last Saturday night. I had a sense this was to be the "last supper," but I'd made that pronouncement before to no avail. Still, somewhere around the ice cream course, I really started to believe. And by one the next morning, against the backdrop of a very bad beach movie, Adam had started to believe, too.

We called my folks just before three, and took off for the hospital at 3:15, tearing through the empty downtown with visions of a fourth child arriving en route spurring us on. Ultimately, the baby wasn't born for another twelve hours, just in time for game three of the Leafs-Canes series.

She was huge (9 lbs, 12 oz) and lovely, with smoky eyes blinking at us from under a mess of dark hair.

And now we're home, a little more than a week after the fact, adjusting to life with this bridge-tableful of children. Thankfully, new babies sleep a lot, which means Kai's participation in our life thus far has mostly been a matter of the older kids falling over each other to hold her and kiss her. Oh, and then there's the challenge that comes with filling apple juice containers and pushing backyard swings and overseeing piano practise with a wailing baby in my arms.

And the logistics of hauling four children about are proving trying, whether it be in and out of the minivan or negotiating our loaner triple stroller through the city streets.

But we're surviving so far. And each new day is an adventure. Over the course of the journey, I plan to indulge every kind offer of assistance from friends and relatives. I plan to make abundant use of the local food-delivery establishments in our neighbourhood. I plan to turn our backyard into a haven of fun for children, since the chances of our considerable familial assemblage venturing too far from it are slim, at best. And I plan to savour every possible moment (at least the moments that I'm not sodden with despair over the impossibility of it all) with my wonderful heap of children.

TO MALINDI, AT AGE FOUR

Dear, sweet Malindi,

Here you are, four years into the game. Hard to believe our sweet second baby, with the cradle-cap scalp and stork-bitten forehead and insanely tangled mess of back-of-head hair is now a little girl. Poised to enter junior kindergarten. Long of leg and mischievous of temperament.

How has it been, my love, to be a middle child? To bring up the rear (at least until your brother and baby sister came along) behind Kenya? Is that what's made you such a spirited, insistent, immovable force of girl? It's hard never to win the race, isn't it, my love? Hard to be sandwiched between such a victorious older sister and such a charming younger brother. And then the baby came, and you were squeezed even more.

You love to scream and to raise the roof with your efforts to be heard. To be responded to. To be noticed, for God's sake. Nothing's sweeter, as far as you're concerned, than pushing us to the very limits of tolerance. Daring us to lose it. Flirting with disaster. To you, my lovely, that kind of attention equals good attention. Somehow, you've learned that this is the point of childhood.

Just the same, you have a stillness to you, my lovely Malindi, that the others don't. You are patient and, for all your carryings-on, your temper is always contained well beneath the surface. You can play forever on your own, a sad legacy of a multiple-child family, perhaps, but useful just the same. And you do have goodness in you. It lurks around your edges, spilling out when you're not paying attention and working to keep the bad-girl schtick in play. One day this week, you gave your arch-enemy Finn your new baton to keep him entertained, even though you'd barely had a chance yet to enjoy it yourself.

You love kitty cats. And your best friend Chloe. You love cake, and parties and books with hidden characters on every page. You love singing to yourself in the back of the car. But mostly you love private time with Mommy. "I don't want Finn there," you will tell me. "Or Kenya either."

We had more than a year of private afternoons before Kai came along, with Kenya at school and Finn at Rita's. You'd lie on my bed and watch cartoons and then eventually wander into my office to ask to do a craft. Sometimes I'd retire with you to the bedroom to watch *A Baby Story*. You always hated when I changed the channel, but you knew the sacrifice was worth it to have Mommy all to yourself. I will always treasure the memory of you during those private afternoons, stretched out on my bed with your arm around the cat.

Happy (belated) birthday, little girl. I love you as much (and more!) as you need me to, and I hope this coming year is our best yet.

THE CORNERS OF MY MIND

Sometimes, when I walk my daughter Kenya to school, holding her hand as she balances along low walls, listening to her dreamy explanations about some part of the *Harry Potter* saga, I get the strangest feeling. For a moment, somewhere between light and shadow, time stands still. Simultaneously, I feel myself being hurled forward and yanked back. I see Kenya as a thirty-five-year-old woman. I see myself as a six-year-old girl.

Memory is a strange and selective machine. It scatters its imprints across a consciousness like footprints in the snow. As the years go by, a path emerges. But it's got no particular rationale.

It's always summer in my memories. It's safe and cozy and coloured right to the edges with new pencil crayons. The soundtrack is laughter: my dad, when I should be sleeping, howling in front of Johnny Carson. My mom, in appreciation of her daughter's emerging kookiness. My childhood has the feeling of promise. It is hopeful. Casting back over it today still makes my adrenaline pump.

It's not so much the individual experiences that I recall about life at Kenya's age. It's an impression. Like the background in a cartoon that the central action plays out against. But there are some specifics, too, like sneaking a peak at the books on my parents' shelves and being completely baffled over the appeal of *The Sun Also Rises* when it was entirely devoid of pictures. I remember getting grounded for "hitchhiking" with a friend (my dad found us with our thumbs out at the edge of the sidewalk) and how I knew I'd done something wrong, but didn't nearly grasp the bigness of the lesson he was trying to impart.

I remember feeling jealous when my mother bought my friend a Sesame Street activity book when she was home sick from kindergarten, getting sent out into the hall in fifth grade for playing the recorder with my nose, burning my hand on a curling iron on my seventh birthday.

Almost three decades later, all of this is gold. Now I can pretty much crawl into my daughter's head at critical junctures, and conjure up her experience from her side of the fence.

Now when she complains about being "cute" instead of "beautiful," I can genuinely feel her pain. Or her joy, as she anticipates a playmate's arrival. Or her confusion when an adult uses a phrase like "he's not the sharpest knife in the drawer." I can remember my own six-year-old self riding that same coaster of wonder, ending each day having learned something new.

On the other hand, this new reality is a killer to my conscience. Because if I can remember being six, well, this kid's going to be able to remember it, too. Up until now, I've been able to write a certain amount of our interactions off to the ephemeral experience of very young childhood. Surely she won't remember the time when she was three, and I promised I wouldn't get mad if she told me the truth about why she bit her friend, and then spanked her when she confessed that she did it because it made her happy. Nope, I won't be getting away with that kind of mixed message anymore. The bad parental choices I make are written in permanent ink now.

And the other downside of this reverie of childhood recall? How it gets smashed to pieces when a passing glance in the bathroom mirror reveals a thirty-five-year-old woman staring back at me. Not the five-year-old, who so recently mastered the art of tying her own shoes. Not the nine-year-old, who turned cartwheels as much as she walked. Not even the seventeen-year-old, who wondered how to handle the flirtatious English teacher. But a moth-eaten, weather-beaten traveller, at least a third of her way into the journey.

Almost two dozen Christmases ago (how could that be?), I got my mom a badge with "Because I'm the mother" printed on it. Somehow, in all the moves since then, that pin has ended up in my cutlery drawer. I caught sight of it recently, and shuddered with the realization that I could wear the thing now — if I so chose.

It's the same dawning horror that regularly washes over me when Kenya has a buddy over and I am forced into the role of "the friend's mother." Now I'm the wise figure of feminine authority who bustles in the kitchen while children spin around her like tops, and who only occasionally interrupts to stick her head into the parlour and ask whether any one needs more sarsaparilla.

No one ever asks the friend's mother to play.

Not that I particularly want to be a kid again. I like late-night television too much. But I will struggle forever with the way time screams past faster with each passing year. I simply cannot believe I am the one signing the permission forms and enforcing the homework now. And how can I be trusted to dole out reasonable advice to a brokenhearted little girl who's been overlooked by a classmate throwing a Micropets party, when I can still remember the same sting of snubbery myself?

When I was younger, I didn't think on my mother's existential presence much. She was just there: pouring my milk, running my baths, tucking me in. But if I ever did stop to consider her, there was never a doubt in my mind that she was The Adult. A big person, to the littler version of me. Almost a different species. She laughed at different jokes, wore different clothes (what was she thinking with that corduroy get-up?) and God knew what she did after we kids went to bed at night. Hers was a mysterious reality that could not be more removed from mine.

But now here I am, three decades and a thousand pounds later, and some fluke of nature has transformed me — of all people! — into The Adult. In some weird *Twilight Zone* twist of plot, my mother, daughter and I have all switched places. It's an achievement that Hallmark has yet to recognize with a card. It qualifies, nonetheless, among the mind-blowing watersheds of one's passage through this place. Like when you buy your first sofa or swallow your first oyster.

The thing is, though, it's still the other me under all of this bad hair and too-many-summers-in-the-sun baked skin. Really, it is! Still the little kid with the crayon in her hand. Which explains why I feel like such a fraud when I'm telling my kids "Because I said so" or "Don't stand up in the bath."

Do other women feel the same way, or am I an emotionally retarded aberration? Better yet, was my own mother faking it too, or did she actually make the transition successfully? Even as I hurtle along the path toward old ladydom — now there will be a transition! — clinging to the sides of my cart and hoping my Diet Coke doesn't spill, I don't suppose I will ever know.

PARENTING 101

For the past several weeks, Adam and I have been taking a course. Not in pottery or Pilates, but in parenting. According to my grandmother, we couldn't be wasting more money if we were taking lessons in the art and science of blowing your nose.

But off we trek every Thursday evening just the same, into the sitting area of a neighbourhood Presbyterian church, to gather with five other equally thriftless couples. Under the tutelage of the "instructor," Joanne, we spill the latest of our parenting challenges onto the grungy carpet and await advice, approval. Understanding. Forgiveness.

Last week, we all nodded sympathetically as Rob and Val shared yet another tale of their tantrum-inclined four-year-old who invariably works himself to such a pitch that he vomits. What to do? Throw the kid a cloth and turn on *Oprah*. "Really?" asks an incredulous Val. "Really," confirms Joanne. You'll be doing him a favour in the long run.

Successful parenting, as it turns out, is largely an exercise in ignoring. If your five-year-old is whining because she can't jump rope as well as her friend, ignore her. If your two-year-old goes ballistic when you refuse the advances of the ice cream truck, ignore her, too. There's only one way to teach your children not to interrupt, snivel and scrap: teleport your weary self to another plane (ideally one bound for Antigua) and totally check out of the drama.

But you need to get a few of the ground rules down first. We spent an evening a couple of weeks back discriminating between consequence and punishment. Mark revealed that when he was a boy, his father's answer to unacceptable behaviour was to send him out to the woodpile with an axe. One glance at Joanne and you know she's thinking Mark's dad was so old-school. A parent's response needs to be a natural followup to the behaviour, she explains. If your kid keeps running into the yard and stomping your petunias, for example, well, maybe he just doesn't get any more garden parties for a while.

The next week, we dissected the subtle shades that distinguish praise from encouragement. This is critical, says Joanne, because if we dwell too thickly in the camp of the former, we'll spawn card-carrying credit junkies who can't get through the day without stroking and attention. Encouragement, on the other hand, puts the satisfaction for a deed back in the hands of the kid. So don't applaud your little darling's scribbling of a horse — ask him if he feels this rendering to be superior to the one he completed yesterday, or invite him to indulge you in an explanation of how he mixed the browns just so.

Our six-year-old Kenya cottoned onto our laboured attempts at this new parenting stratagem right away. I knew it when I failed to respond to the achievement of an independently tied shoe at the end of her leg. "Aren't you going to say, 'You must be very proud of yourself,'" she trilled, in a sing-song voice, "like they taught you at parenting class?"

HAMMY'S ODYSSEY

The hamster was a mistake from the start. When you've got four kids, two cats and a dog, undertaking to care for even one more little life is a serious display of overextension. But I had such fond memories of the little rodents who were my childhood companions that I wanted nothing less for my own little girl. So I'd promised Kenya that, when she turned five, she could have her own hamster.

The day in question arrived, and I took great pleasure in picking the particular ball of fur that would be our pet. And our pet he was (or perhaps mine more than hers, considering the imbalance of care I provided on his behalf), for more than a year. Everybody loved little Hammy. Malindi, for one, loved the way his little legs splayed out when he was dropped from a height onto the carpet. Finn loved how his eyes bulged when you poked them, and how you could squish him in one hand like a hot dog bun. It was in acknowledgement of this fond affection that I allowed Hammy to exist on a low-level shelf, within easy view of the kids.

Then one day it happened. Finnie worked out how to open the cage, and he set our little eiderdown pouf loose upon the world. It was Sunday night when I came upon the empty cage. Hammy could have been gone as many as ten hours by that point. I set up a search party nonetheless, one that included the considerable participation of our cats and our dog. For half an hour, we looked into every warm, dark corner and paused to consider every suspicious sound in our universe. No luck. Hammy would either turn up or he wouldn't, I reasoned, and the children were surprisingly accepting of that. In my gut, I had serious doubts. I'd lost too many little creatures to black holes of my own youth (I kept expecting to come upon some of those tiny carcasses) to hold out much hope.

Four more evenings passed. Then Adam called me down to the basement where he was playing with the kids. "We heard something," he said. "Up there." He indicated the furnace ducts that snaked along the ceiling. I listened, and, sure enough, detected a faint scratching against the metal. We hauled out Adam's toolbox and tried to wrench one piece of duct from the other. But there was no way. These things were built to last. In the end, we threw a couple of carrots down the vent, mercifully remembered to turn the furnace off and all went to bed.

The next day, an overwhelming sense of guilt pushed me to place a few calls of inquiry about the possibility of rescuing our little critter. The gas company said they had no idea. The animal rescue folks suggested we call a duct cleaning place. And I was all set up with an eighty-dollar-an-hour duct cleaner before the guy called me back to make sure I understood the exact ramifications of the extraction. "We'd be vacuuming him out of there, you understand?" he said. "The hamster will die in the process." I cancelled the appointment.

It was Friday now, maybe 130 hours after Hammy had first tasted freedom. Adam and I were watching *Law & Order* in the living room when we heard the scratching again. This time, when we went down to the basement, we came across a little hole in the duct that we hadn't noticed before, plugged up with the same kind of rubber stopper you find in the bottom of a piggy bank. We pried it loose and, sure enough, were rewarded with the sight of little feet scampering across the opening. Because the hole was too small, we had to cut the metal away and peel it back. Then I held up a cucumber stick that the famished hamster immediately locked onto and I was able to lower him through, teeth first. For one horrifying moment, we wondered if we were in fact pulling another rodent out from our vents. But it was Hammy, his fur hot-air blasted from the furnace, one eye mysteriously squished shut, seriously skinny. But alive.

We transported him back to his cage, filled the place with food and water and crossed our fingers that he would still be around when the kids woke up. He was and, several weeks after the Great Escape, Hammy continues to amaze us with his survival techniques. He's still principally my responsibility. He's still the object of questionable affection with the kids. But he's no longer living on a low-level shelf.

Princess Finn

All political correctness aside, I must confess that I'm starting to wonder about my son's fascination with girly stuff. Almost as soon as those fat little hands could reach for things, Finn was keen to get them on objects normally designated part of the feminine oeuvre. He loves hairbands and barrettes. He applies both to his brilliant blond locks quite adeptly, and then struts about the place, announcing, Hat. Sometimes, a hairband will fall down in front of his eyes, and he'll look like that guy from *Star Trek*.

In his sisters' room, there's a tub of dress-up clothes, just spilling over with tulle and chiffon. There are scarves and gloves and a bewildering halter top that came with a grass skirt courtesy of Uncle Mike's trip to Hawaii. All of it is fodder for young Finnie, who tends to put skirts over his head and then buck about madly when he can't pull the delicate silky tank tops over his muscular calves. Getting clothes right side up is something my son has yet to master.

And then there's the footwear. There is nothing this little boy likes so much as to stumble about the place in his sisters' dress-up shoes. He has a particular fondness for the pink leopard print, but is generally not too choosy. Sometimes he struggles to jam his porky little piggies into some of the mules, but he's largely self-sufficient for a two-year-old left to his own devices with a pair of pumps. My main concern (aside from metatarsalgia, plantar fasciitis and hammertoes) is that he'll come tumbling down the stairs. I'm also none too fond of the occasional encounter his plastic heels make with my own bare feet. But I must say, he does look smashing. Especially when he pairs the shoes with shades and a great handbag.

With all of this in his history, it shouldn't have surprised me in the least when Finn went for the makeup. I keep my meagre collection of cosmetics in a cup on the bathroom window ledge. I suppose I could move it, but it's just so convenient for me there. It is, too, for a little boy who's been hoisting himself up onto the toilet seat since he was mobile. Which explains why Finn occasionally shows up with great streaks of mascara across his face and eyeliner lining everything but his eyes.

He is a glamourpuss, to be sure, my boy is. And with his impossibly long lashes and flaxen hair he could probably put most little girls in the neighbourhood to shame (particularly in that little taffeta number). Indeed, at a birthday party this summer, he did just that, when the mother wheeled out little rose-coloured tutus and pink T-shirts with "princess" spelled out in rhinestones across the front. It would have cost too much to have a single "prince" shirt done up, she apologized, and so she hoped I wouldn't mind if Finn — the single male guest — had to wear the girls' garb, too. "Mind?" I asked, as my little slugger appeared on the back deck in his skirt and tiara. He was carrying a princess sceptre in one hand and a gold clutch purse in the other. "What's to mind?"

PERFECT PARTY PURSUITS

My eldest is about to turn seven and the heat is on to produce the perfect party. Not that Kenya is getting at all warm. I'm the one in the kitchen here, trying to whip up the seared-salmon-with-roasted-tomatillo-coulis of kids' birthday fetes. Because, let's face it, these parties are as much about impressing the kids as the fancy cookies we serve at the playgroups are.

When I turned seven, my mom invited a few neighbourhood children over to our house. We gathered in the living room and played Pin the Tail on the Donkey and Simon Says. We ate hot dogs and cake, and sat in a circle while I opened my gifts. Everybody went home with a pinwheel, a Tootsie Roll and the memory of a great afternoon. But that sweet, simple celebration just wouldn't cut it today. Not unless the donkey was the real deal, and the part of Simon was played, by special arrangement, by Johnny Depp.

I have a friend whose kid is a Harry Potter nut. For her daughter's birthday this year, she transformed each room in the house into a different store from Diagon Alley. She stayed up night after night sewing black capes and pointy hats for each of the guests to purchase from Madame Malkin's Robes for All Occasions. She had her husband drill holes in a dozen wooden dowels so that the kids could personalize their magic "wands" at Ollivander's Wand Shoppe, by stuffing them with unicorn tail hairs, dragon scales and fairy eyes. She even made a seven- (count them: seven) layer birthday cake in the shape of a sorting hat. At the end of it all, each of the party attendees trotted home with their own snitch ball and the bottle of butter beer they had cooked up with Professor Snape in the dungeon. Not too shabby. This mom should have no problem showing her face around the schoolyard.

I know another woman who routinely rents one of those huge jumping castles for her kids' party guests to go nuts in. It costs a few bucks, but it's a guaranteed winner. Sometimes, there are pony rides. Magicians. Face painters. Rock-climbing. Mad scientists who make putty and set off rockets. Once, I heard about a mom hiring The Wiggles to perform in the backyard, but that might have been an urban myth of the kids' party circuit. In any event, it all makes its way back to the guests' mothers, who watch with dread as the party-planning bar inches ever higher.

For Kenya, I'm having a couple of "entertainers" drop by with their disco ball and boom box. The kids will be instructed on the finer points of hip hop to the stylin' sounds of Britney and Justin. There will be finger foods and punch. Hair and cosmetic services will be provided prior to the dancing. At the end, the kids will go home with nifty plastic cases filled with little pots of make-up and sparkly jewellery. The whole thing will cost me in the neighbourhood of $300. But it will be worth every dime to see Kenya's shining face as the celebration swirls around her. And that's what it's all about, after all. Not what the other moms will have to say about me and my little party at their coffee klatches.

But I do hope the kids remember to tell their mommies about the disco ball...

TO KENYA, AT AGE SEVEN

Dear sweet, complicated Kenya,

Today, I watched you, my newly seven-year-old girl, after I'd crossed the street beside you, as you ran along the sidewalk toward your piano teacher's house. And I was amazed at how tiny you still are. I think I'm sometimes deceived by the bigness of your presence in my life. You're loud and brash and, from all accounts, *at least* seven. You're full of opinions. And attitude. Often angry. And sometimes incredibly silly. So when I saw your little body, clad in overalls and a turtleneck covered in puppydogs, I was completely caught off guard by the little girl I'd forgotten was still here. But I was so grateful to come across her. Seven years, Kenya! Can you believe it? How far we've come. How far we still have to go.

I am so, so proud of the person you've become, my love. You're sensitive. And self-conscious. Considerate. Delightfully crazy. You're the dreamiest creature I've met, giving even your dazed daddy a run for his money. You wander about the place, a toothbrush in your hand, wondering what it was you were off to do. You forget to bring your homework home almost every single night.

In many ways, you are typical first-child material. You're calm and sensible. Often shy. Very independent. Except for occasions of astounding drifty-ness, you're highly trustworthy. You're so mature and wise, that I sometimes think your mind and soul are just waiting for your body to catch up. But you play your cards too close to your vest for my liking. I wish you'd let me in more. You're cautious. Sometimes, I know, you have questions. But you so rarely share them with me. That is why it is so important for you to choose your friends wisely, because I fear they will provide much more counsel than I.

I wish our lives weren't such a scramble. I wish I didn't have to tell you six times to put on your jacket or brush your teeth. I wish we had more time for cuddling and less time for nagging. Piano practice, dictée recital, art class, French books, English books, and so on and so on. Don't you wish we could just lie in bed together the way we used to? When you were just a tiny thing, my very first little love, and we huddled in the stillness and wondered where we were going together?

I remember how your life opened up after that, and how the centre of your world shifted from me to you. I remember how I marvelled at the little universe you were creating for yourself and how my place in it was relegated ever closer to the periphery. Now, I honestly don't know how you spend most of your day. What thoughts make their way through that magnificent brain as you sit in your classrooms and race around during your recesses. Dear Kenya, I miss you. Wish you were here.

But I do love what I can glean from the sidelines. What you let slip when you think I'm barely listening. What I fasten on to when you open up above the din of our family life and allow, for example, that Liam had hurt your feelings when he insulted your new birthday diary. I'm prepared now to get real with you, because I recognize that the incredible constraints of our existence simply don't allow me to get away with pat little homilies any longer. So I tell you to insult Liam in the same spirit. When he says, "Nice diary...not!" you tell him, "Nice face...not!" I mean it. And you can see that.

I'm tired of "playing" mom, and am ready to just be one. Anyway, my dear, sweet, more-than-seven-year-old. I told you the other day that you were "my star," and I pinned a star from a Christmas cushion onto your shirt. You lost the star after that, and later showed up with one that had been glued to your bedroom wall. It fell off the wall, you said. And I looked at you hard because I knew it wasn't the truth. And you knew I knew. In my room after that, you came to tell me you'd lied, and that you'd ripped the star down. It was a tiny moment in our crazy life, but it meant the world to me. Thank you for coming clean, Kenya Lee. I hope you always will. And, just so you know, you always will be my star.

REGISTRATION DAY

I brought the portable phone up from the kitchen, unplugged the cellphone from its charger, delivered my MasterCard up to the bedside table, set the alarm for 6:59 and pressed the phone number onto the keypad so I could start the day in "redial" mode. "I will get through on the first try," I muttered to myself as I snuggled down into my pillows, cradling my phones. Adam looked at me anxiously. When sleep finally claimed me, I had a dream about bells.

The next morning — registration day for spring and summer Parks and Rec programs — dawned with new promise. I pushed my first "redial" before the alarm even went off.

After a while, a busy signal takes on a certain haunting rhythm. Its insistent beat can lull you into immobilization if you're not careful, and you'll forget to hang up and surprise yourself, minutes later, to realize you're still listening — eyes fixed on some spot in the distance — to its bleating tones. Or else you'll do some other silly thing, like press redial before hanging up the phone, and that will cause you to actually have to punch the whole ten digits in again.

My friend Sheila almost always gets through on the first try. She'll ring through just as the clock turns over to 7:00 am, and the cheerful Parks and Rec rep will fulfill her every heart's desire. At a certain point during my busy signal sessions, my call-waiting will beep, and I'll flip over to hear her breathless tales of how easy it was to get her daughter into every program we'd mapped out the night before. "Did you get in?" she'll ask at last. "Nope," I'll sigh. "Not yet."

On this particular almost-spring Wednesday morning, I worked the phones for close to five hours. I moved from my bedroom to the office in a relentless pursuit of the sound of ringing at the other end of the line. It was noon before I heard it. I horrified myself by almost hanging up out of habit.

Needless to say, every single one of my first choices was full. My plan to align my daughters' swimming lessons so that we didn't have to hustle to the pool twice in one week died in the water early on. In fact, I wasn't able to get Malindi into swimming at all, and Kenya had to settle for a class with seven other kids at 7:15 in the evening (as opposed to the tidy four-person, 4:15 class we were shooting for).

What's more, the dance camp Sheila had enrolled her daughter in was full up. I put Kenya on the waiting list, then went ahead and enrolled her in a theatre camp. Times of crisis call for executive decisions, after all. I called Sheila and told her of the revised plan. But by the time she got through to make the switch, that one was full, too. She put her daughter on the waiting list, and proceeded to enroll her in a third camp, this one for music.

"Call them right back," she said, "and get Kenya in the music camp. There are still spaces."

I sighed, and reboarded the redial treadmill. It was afternoon by now, and most other mothers had either gotten through, or taken their own lives out of frustration. It took a mere twenty minutes for me to surface from busy-signal hell this time. When I did, I took Kenya out of the theatre camp she was in, pulled her off the dance camp waiting list, enrolled her in music camp, hung up the phone on the by-now considerably less cheerful Parks and Rec rep, and cried like a baby. In that order.

That night, I dreamed of busy signals.

MAGNIFICENT MALINDI

Malindi is our pointy child. All her edges are sharp. She's as lovely as a princess — so long as it's one with devious eyes and scratchy fingernails and angular limbs. But the sharpness is more about personality than looks. She has a way of exploding into a situation like a nail bomb, and then slicing her crafty way out of it like a jackknife. Her laugh is more of a cackle than a belly burst. Her voice is often shrill. She's as manipulative as a politician (but several times more cuddly). She will cry for what she wants, and then flip into song when she gets it. And she's not above playing one family member against another, if it means she gets to come out on top.

But she is also a passionate soul, my Malindi. She has adored pussycats, pretty shoes and her pacifier forever. She loves to run and to dance, and all things with sugar featured prominently in their ingredients (an interest in brushing her teeth, however, does not follow). And she's a clown, who couldn't be more aware of her charms if they were read off a scroll. "I'm funny," she'll announce, to no one in particular. Or "I'm cute," piped up from the backseat of the minivan. No one dares to dispute any of her claims.

Sometimes, she'll make strange announcements, apropos of nothing at all, like, "I'm thinking about penguins" or "You're in my day!" And she has always had her own little language of self-conscious Malindi-isms ("keppage" for "ketchup," for example, and "pickage" for "picture") that never fail to make me laugh.

Today, she removed her pacifier from her mouth just long enough to proclaim, "Mommy, you will be a singer when you grow up." But what will she be, I wonder? It hurts my head to project that many years forward, but even when I force myself, I come up empty.

When I think of the future, my view is more short-sighted with Malindi than it is with her older sister. It's less about what she'll do with her life and what she'll be when she grows up as it is musings about what kind of kid she'll be next year. After all, who could contemplate the future that awaits a feisty, cuts-like-a-knife personality whose daddy identified as a "ball of intention" when she was a mere eighteen months old? She is too many things to fasten in on one.

And as for me, I will stand by and watch with wonder as the mystery unfolds. And I will reflect on how wonderful my time with my sharp, pointy second child has been up till now (except perhaps that day when she pitched such a fit at McDonald's she got keppage in my hair).

FIERCE FRIENDS

My daughter Kenya is my best friend in the world. She is also my worst enemy. My greatest joy and my deepest sorrow. My affirmation of victory; my confirmation of defeat. Still just seven, Kenya has the power to rip into me emotionally and uncover my most tender parts. Sometimes, she will tell me she loves me when I am rubbing her back at bedtime and I will be grateful for the cloak of darkness so she won't see the tears welling in my eyes. And then the next morning, she'll ignite like a fuse when I insist that she brush her teeth before heading downstairs. "I hate you," she'll hiss.

And I'll feel the tears welling again.

I remember when Kenya was a baby, newly arrived in our lives. She was our first child, and was thus blessed with all the attendant stresses and anxieties that first children typically are. I remember how one thought kept haunting me: what if Kenya wasn't happy with the family fate had placed her with? What if, somewhere in the folds of her baby brain, she was experiencing disappointment about her lot, and wishing wordlessly that she'd ended up with a better deal?

Ever since, Kenya has been capable of undermining my confidence like no one else. To compensate, I get aggressive. And then the sparks really fly. If butting heads were an Olympic sport, Kenya and I both would win places on our national team. She and I yank on each other's nerves a dozen times a day. As a rule, I don't believe in spanking. But all of the times I've been pushed to the edge and across it, Kenya's been by my side.

What's more, it's around her that I frequently feel like a fraud mother, playing a speaking part in a drama that should have gone to somebody more obviously suited to it, like my friend Susan, or even Sharon Osbourne. "Get up to your room," I'll sputter in an unconvincing voice, and I can just imagine the director sending the script back for a rewrite, and then whispering to his assistant that I should be recast.

Some areas of our lives are more incendiary than others. Take hair care, for example. Kenya and I have a fight about this messy subject almost every day. It's become a power struggle so pivotal to our relationship that it's a wonder neither of us has whacked the other with a brush. The other day, I was out for a walk with a friend and our kids. Her two children were walking ahead of us, and I pointed out to Kenya how lovely Chloe's hair looked.

"Why is it that she lets her mommy brush her hair, and you never will?" I asked, just spoiling for a fight.

"Why do you have to compare me to everybody else?" Kenya spat back.

It wasn't the reaction I was expecting, and I had to push down the rising guilt in my throat to get my next line out.

"Because everybody else looks so neat and pretty, and you look like something the cat's dragged in."

It was a cheap shot, but slicing each other up with zingers like this is typical for us in these prickly encounters. Like terrible enemies do.

My daughter stomped away with a signature "Harrumph," leaving me with the sad knowledge that I had once again failed to keep my emotions in check.

"I'm sorry," I whispered into Kenya's hair (which really wasn't that tangled at all), after rushing to catch up with her and wrap my arms around her tummy.

"OK," she said. And we held onto each other tight. Like best friends do.

Loving a Son

When I found out that the third child I was carrying in my womb was not a girl, I panicked. All I had known up to that point was the female specimen. I was completely in the dark when it came to boys.

Over the next several months, I polled every son's mother I knew. I was in desperate pursuit of some reason — any reason — to be hopeful. After all, a boy, with apologies to Adam, my father and my brother, is a foreign beast. My little guy, I was convinced, was going to be my most difficult and least delightful child of all. I couldn't have been more mistaken.

My son Finn has filled out the edges of my life like nothing else. In the years since he burst into our lives, I have come to appreciate that mommies of sons are incredibly blessed. How lucky they are to know what it's like to love a little boy.

Right from the start, Finn was a keeper. Adam and I would come together in the evening and, with our sweet boy baby between us in the bed, fasten on him and marvel. We would share stories of exquisite moments from the day (like how he was clever enough to figure out how to unfasten the Velcro tabs on his diapers, or how he would visit me in the bathtub, and lay his head sideways on the tub until I kissed it). And then we would say one more time what a handsome infant he was, and how sweet his little dimple is when he smiles. (I remember, in the days after he was born, e-mailing my parents on their holiday down east. The baby's got a dimple, I wrote, and then covered the screen with exclamation points. I'd always wanted a child with a dimple-cheeked smile.)

Loving my son is the most pure and sincere thing I have ever done. He's a genuine soul whose presence in our lives is so massive it's impossible to remember a time when he wasn't around. And I do mean massive. Everything about my boy is big: a big head of sunshine-coloured hair; big eyes, framed by wildly long lashes; big laughter. He's hugely happy from the moment he wakes in the morning until his last guffaw of the night (most recently, born of a joke about penises, shared with Malindi).

But a boy is a bombast, and as much as concerned friends tried to shield my anxious, pregnant self from that, there's no denying that reality. When he was still just a baby, Finn would astound fellow park-goers with moxy enough to tackle the highest slide in the place, and then come down it as fast as a sudden rainstorm. As soon as he could walk, the couch became his balance beam and the bookcase his climbing frame. If we let him, Finn would mow the lawn and paint the bathroom and drive the van.

Eventually, though, even a boy is capable of succumbing to stillness. Sleep claims my boy quickly, and he generally accepts the arrival of his bedtime without fuss. If I'm lucky, and Kai has fallen asleep before him, I get to indulge an old passion of mine and share with him his twin-bed journey into dreamland.

Delighted to have me to himself, Finn will gather an enormous stack of books and climb into my lap. We'll work our way through every one, me reading and turning the pages, him lifting the flaps and stroking the fuzzy bits. Then he'll hunker down under his fat duvet and I'll hand him Bee-Zip, his giant plush bee. "I don't want to hug him tonight," my fickle boy might say, and push him to the side of the bed.

When I jump up to flip the light switch, I know he's holding his breath in the darkness until I return.

We'll lie in silence for a bit, my ears listening for the slowing of his breath, the setting-in of slumber. "I love you, Mommy," he'll say, his lovely voice reaching out for me in the quiet. "I love you, too," I'll say. It is his favourite refrain, his verbal expression of all that I see in his eyes. He tells me often, to make sure, I sense, that I understand just how deeply the sentiments run. My fingers will find his and hold on.

At last his breath will adopt a rhythm. His grip on my hand will loosen, and I will know sleep has claimed him. Finn is a deep and serious sleeper, so taking my leave is fairly easily done. At the door, I'll look back at him, the shuttered moonlight casting light stripes across his face. To his dozing brain, Mommy is still there, snuggled in beside him, a comforting bookend to Bee-Zip. I hope the illusion gives him peace. I want him to know that I will always be there. Not in a creepy kind of way, like the mother who hauls a ladder to her grown son's house and then breaks into his bedroom to watch him sleep. Just in a reassuring kind of way. Like a fat duvet in the nighttime. Or a Bee-Zip at his side — even if he doesn't give him a hug.

Rites of Passage

I was never a Brownie. I always regarded the little girls in those stiff brown uniforms spotted with fat badges with some curiosity. They were part of a club to which I had no membership.

Fast-forward three decades.

Whatever it was that inspired me to sign Kenya on with this enigmatic sorority is still up for grabs. Probably, like so many things, it was just a case of going with the flow. All of my friends seemed to be enrolling their little girls with this church-basement phenomenon. What's a mother to do but join the flock? And last week, my daughter became a full-fledged Brownie. The old-fashioned brown regalia has given way to more modern orange-and-brown garb. But the necktie and badge-pocked sash are still there. And so is the frighteningly cult-like atmosphere of the whole affair.

With the parents gathered at one end of the meeting space, cameras in hand, the indoctrination ceremony began. All told, some twenty young girls were minted that night. And the ceremony left me feeling just as much in the dark as it did a generation ago. It was almost an out-of-body experience sitting there, watching my seven-year-old march through the paces that would secure her entry into this ancient society.

First, a gaggle of Brownies acted out an abridged version of the "Brownie Story." Here, two little girls learn the value of lending a hand when their grandmother shares a tale about invisible creatures who help with chores when no one is watching. The girls head into the woods near their home looking for one of these useful little beings, only to realize upon seeing their reflections in a pond that they — themselves — are "brownies." It's a bit of a stretch, and the mark of a poorly crafted story was not lost on the parents in the crowd. Some rolled their eyes with the ridiculousness of it all. Most just looked confused.

Next came the swearing in. The Brownies were divided into several groups, each with its own symbol and clumsy song. Kenya is a Leprechaun: Happy Leprechauns are we, helping friends and family. A second-year Brownie with swingy straight hair and brown knee socks led her by the hand around a horseshoe of cross-legged girls, all of them singing an incessant ditty about how "the fun is just beginning" for these little innocents, as they pledged their lives to the force of brown. As the ceremony unfolded, I was increasingly apprehensive of this whole crazy idea. The thought of leaping up from my wooden chair and yanking my daughter out of the Brownie web, up the church stairs and into freedom actually crossed my brain. But Spotted Owl fixed me with a glare (I swear) and I remained strangely rooted.

On the floor at the end of a path made up of the "stepping stones" of Browniedom (The Brownie Promise, the Brownie Law, the Brownie Motto, the Brownie Sign and Handshake, the Brownie tie and proof of attendance at a minimum of three meetings), was a mirror. Here, the girls were to reenact the age-old observance of recognizing their own Brownieness in the pond's reflection. Beyond that, stood Brown Owl, an imposing figure whose real name, I would guess, remains a mystery to most of the little girls over whom she towers.

"Brown Owl," said the older girl. "Kenya would like to be a Brownie."

Brown Owl thanked Kenya's "sponsor," and then instructed Kenya to recite the Brownie Promise. She did so, in a tiny voice that made me wince with the imposed gravity of it all, and then she and the head bird exchanged the Brownie handshake (a left-hand grab with the right hand raised with two fingers upright).

At the end, I was invited up to tie Kenya's scarf around her neck with a reef knot. And then that was it. My oldest daughter was officially "made," and there ain't no unmaking in this tightknit organization. Back at my seat, a slew of emotions rushed over me. And then the father of one of Kenya's friends nudged me and broke the reverie. "It's only a short distance from this, to this," he said, first making the Brownie sign, and then shooting his hand up in a Heil Hitler salute.

Thanks. Just what I needed to hear.

To Malindi, at Age Five

Dear Malindi,

Here's what I know so far.

More than five years ago, we brought our second baby, wrapped in hospital-issue fleece, home. Deep into the toddler years with your older sister, we were absolutely thrilled to return to the newborn stage with you (even if it did mean wearing bras to bed again). Your evolution from those early days has been fluid. Seamlessly, my little Mole has grown from wiggly, heavy-of-head baby, indignant at the silly hats her parents put her in, to whip-smart, apple-sweet little girl (still wearing the occasional silly hat). And what a trip it's been.

From the start, Malindi, you have made me laugh. With your older sister having laid tight claim to the more serious part in our family, you took on the funny role, providing comic relief at every turn. To you, life's absurdities are self-evident, and you celebrate them often with a sharp, staccato guffaw that cuts through the heaviness of any moment.

Your mind is always on the move. Indeed, one day not so long ago, you confided that. "My brain is always thinking of things, even when I don't want it to be."

"I'd rather be a girl than a boy," you tell me, "because boys have strings hanging out of their vaginas."

Or, "I have a great idea for making a cookie," and then you launch into an explanation that is so incredibly detailed that a person can't help but lose track partway through.

Rare is the moment, my little love, when words are not spilling from your gap-toothed mouth. "I'm a Gemini," you'll offer as defenseless proof, when the matter of your talkativeness is brought up.

But all is not chuckles and chatter with you. There are unpleasant encounters, too, during which your forged-iron will surfaces and the easygoing second child takes a powder. "I don't have to go pee," you'll insist, your enormous brown eyes bulging from the effort of it all. Your fashion choices are just as inflexible. The daily ritual of picking a "Malindi outfit" is about as welcome around here as a visit to the dentist. Mommy and Daddy rush about the second floor, keeping busy with other early-morning distractions in a furious effort not to be the one on call when the last duty remaining is to help Malindi choose her clothes.

It has to be a skirt. That's a given. But the top, tights and accessories are subjects of much debate. "This one?" we'll ask, holding up piece after piece of neglected clothing (the constant stream of big-sister hand-me-downs has crowded your drawers enormously). And don't even think of suggesting the hot-pink tunic with the word "CAT" spelled across its front. "People will laugh at me," you'll protest (despite your eventual acceptance of the leopard-print regalia, complete with a chokerleash and a request for animal-ear ponytails). Inevitably, the one parent will lose her patience and stomp out of the bedroom. You'll remain on your bed in a heap of despair until the other parent takes pity on you. Such are the less than delightful moments with you, my love.

But, mostly, it's French toast and sunshine. It's blown kisses and blown hugs (your invention) from the base of the kindergarten steps. It's an endless stream of made-up dances, pranced around the family room in the genuine conviction of grace. It's giggling trips behind the couch and under the zebra rug. It's joyful discoveries of Xs engraved on the pavement, and snowflakes that have retained their shape on the lawn. And it's more smiles and sweet expressions of love ("But I love you more, Mommy!") than I could ever give thanks for.

That is what I know so far.

BEDTIME

I sleep around.

My mother hates it, and Adam does, too. But there isn't much I can do about it. After all, I've got four kids, and any bookmaker would tell you that the odds of them all sleeping through the night, every night, are extremely slim. Several of them require my presence to make the journey back to slumber. So I go where I'm needed, often in a groggy haze, occasionally bumping into door frames en route. Indeed, I frequently make several revisions to my sleep plans over the course of a single nocturnal period. That's where the sleeping around comes in. But Adam has been known to do his share of sleeping around, too, so he can hardly point the finger at me alone. Ours is a house of extraordinary bedtime hijinks.

Take last night, for example.

We trudged upstairs at about 7:45, heavy with the weight of the getting-ready-for-bed toil that lay ahead. First, every kid had to be stripped down, and their discarded clothes had to be dealt with. We don't have a laundry chute in our house, but I like to pretend that we do (eventually, I will gather up the collection of dirty pants and balled-up underwear that accumulates in the landing, and throw it down the next set of stairs, into the basement).

Then it was on to the business of finding appropriate nighttime attire (Kenya's are never cozy enough, she complains; Malindi's are never pretty). Adam generally tackles Kai here, because he's got more strength to deal with her muscular resistance to being at all tampered with, at a bodily level. I'll help Finn, who has become increasingly convinced of his prowess putting on his own clothes. While I appreciate his efforts, they generally result in upside-down pyjama tops and extreme frustration.

But toothbrushing is the most dreaded of the ready-for-bed exercises, and Adam and I parry and thrust around its imperative like a couple of nervous fencers.

"I'll take Finn if you do Malindi," he offered last night, knowing he was getting the better end of the deal.

"OK," I said, "but you do Kai."

"I don't do Kai," he said, restating an unfortunate precedent that was established (weak moment: my part) way back when I first took on the role of wrestling my way into a frantic baby's mouth with a toothbrush.

The deal was struck then, for another night, and we all set about our dental-care tasks. Inevitably, Adam had to drag Finn out from under his bed, Malindi shrieked several times during the process, and someone got kicked by Kai's flailing feet as I held her across my lap in our tiny bathroom. All in a night's work.

And then the deed was done, and it was time for a book.

For Finn, book time is a just another name for horseplay. He uses the occasion to clamber up the leg of the girls' bunk beds, and to leap from their toy chest onto the bottom mattress. Kai, meanwhile, busies herself emptying out her sisters' toy tubs, and crawling back and forth to my breast for a snack, uprooting a snuggled-up Malindi with each arrival. The older girls will take a passing interest in the story, but they generally end up in a scrap about something, whispered in increasingly sharp tones across my dramatic reading until I stop and demand order.

Kenya and Malindi were restless last night, and wanted a second chapter of *The Frog Princess* before lights out. (Kenya gets frustrated with the way that each chapter ends on a dangling note. She wants resolution, and hates not knowing what's going to happen next.) I indulged them with a few more pages. But then it was time to go.

Lights out in the big girls' room signals bedtime for Finn and Kai. Adam and I divide and conquer here, with him attending the former to his twin bed, to lie in silence alongside him until he falls asleep; and me transporting the latter into our bed, for enough nursing to make her eyelids close.

At last, we exited our respective rooms, blinking at the light, giddy with our freedom, and headed downstairs. There, we shared a meal that was only occasionally interrupted by the appearance of little girls complaining that their tummies hurt, or that the other stole all the blankets or that the room was too dark for sleep. Eventually, Adam stomped up the stairs and into their room to give a "final warning," complete with a vague threat of punishment if they didn't keep quiet and get to sleep.

When we finally retired for the evening, we were exhausted. Because Kai had fallen asleep before Adam left Finn (and I didn't want to disturb them by transplanting her to the crib that resides in the same room as Finn's bed), I'd left her on our bed. I picked her up when we arrived, took her to her crib, crossed my fingers that the move wouldn't be too hard on her REMs, and tiptoed out of the room. Adam, meanwhile, switched on *Letterman*.

About an hour later, Kai woke up. I rushed to grab her, lest her cries wake up her room partner. But it was too late. Finnie wandered into the hallway less than a minute later. "Mommy?" he said. Adam sighed heavily, and then got out of our bed and went back in with his son. I nursed Kai in our bed and we eventually all fell asleep.

A couple of hours after that, Malindi got up. Her tummy still hurt, she said, from the side of my bed. Could she sleep with me? Because Adam had since returned to my side, I left Kai with him and followed Malindi back into her bed. I must have been there just an hour before Kai started crying again. In despair, she had trailed into Finn's room, thinking I was there. This, of course, yanked Finn back into wakefulness. He passed Kai in the hall on his way to our room. With Finn back in our bed with Adam, I scooped up Kai and went to Finn's bed. Malindi, thankfully, had since fallen asleep.

In the morning, Kenya came looking for me. "Why are you here?" she asked, when she finally found me in Finn's room, deeply sleeping under his duvet.

"I can't remember," I told her. And I couldn't.

THE BABYSITTER DANCE

From the moment you push a child out into the waiting hands of another person (hopefully some kind of trained professional), you commit yourself to being at least somewhat dependent on other people in the care and raising of your offspring.

And that can be both blessing and curse. The blessing part is easy enough. A blessed night out at the flicks while a spotty-faced Mary Poppins puts your little darlings to bed, for one. More than twelve seconds of uninterrupted conversation with another person who doesn't require you to constantly refill his juice container, for another. And a chance to remember life when it didn't revolve around diaper changes and Duplo.

But the curse lurks around every corner. Take the corner I negotiated last night, for example, when I picked up a telephone message from my increasingly fragile daytime babysitter, who was calling to say she'd pulled a muscle in her back lifting her luggage and would need "several weeks" to recover. This is the same reliable soul who, in the four-month course of our employ, has had two debilitating bouts of the flu, has missed a flight back from Los Angeles, has had to stay home and care for her sick daughter, twice, and who once phoned to request a day off just to "fix up" her new apartment.

Aaargh.

In the seven years since I have been availing myself of childcare help, I've been through the wars and back. A couple of our nannies have been dreams; the rest have been nightmares. The current sitter with the frail lumbar muscles should not have to bear the cross for those that came before her (and she'd no doubt buckle under the strain). There was the one who caught her fingers in the car door (but who showed up after her respite with nary a scratch on her hand). There were two whose suddenly ill brothers in Montreal required their sisters' immediate assistance. And there was the sitter we hired on a Friday to start on the Monday who simply didn't show up, and whose phone number had mysteriously gone out of service.

I, of course, am completely at the mercy of all of these women. They might be out dancing (as I suspected my current nightmare was when her answering machine picked up my return call yesterday), but there's not much I can do but stand mutely by, hoping she has a change of heart. Or back, as the case may be.

It was a major triumph for me last year when I was able to catapult Kenya across the childcare finish line. Full-time school means no more babysitting in this house. In junior kindergarten, Malindi's just a year-and-a-half from that same milestone. But the way I keep pumping these kids out, I am forever nudging my eventual freedom from all childcare hassles further and further down the road.

In the meantime then, it falls to me to scramble — once again — for a plan B.

Plan Bs are the stock-in-trade at our house, which has seen too many nights of parental midnight oil-burning, as Adam and I struggle to piece together the puzzle of our childcare needs. If Kenya stays at school for lunch on Tuesdays and Thursdays, and if Malindi can spend one morning a week at her friend's, and if Finn goes back into nursery school three days a week, and if Kai could just take longer naps...maybe we could make it work. Maybe. Or maybe my mom could spare us one afternoon, and Adam could go into work late two mornings, and Finn could sit in front of a Wiggles tape and Kai could spend some quality time in her Jolly Jumper...

Eventually — inevitably — we throw up our hands and decide there's nothing for it but to craft yet another irresistible ad for the classifieds, and to embark once again on the Meet the Nannies treadmill. It's an eighty-nine-dollar crapshoot that sends a steady stream of caregiving hopefuls into our midst. With any luck, the next one will have a sense of loyalty that's as strong as her lower back. And vice versa.

TO KENYA, AT AGE EIGHT

Dear Kenya Lee,

Happy eighth birthday. I love being your mommy. I love walking home from school with you, and hearing about how the audition for drama club went, or what Aaron did to get bawled out by the teacher. I love sitting at the kitchen table with you in the late afternoon and sharpening your pencils and watching you work out fractions and write stories about pioneer life. I love coming upon one of your charts, detailing the physical characteristics and particular attributes of each of your Groovy Girls.

When I am with you I am, on some level, eight years old again, playing "pet store" and sharing the magic trick with the five-dollar bill. And other times, I am surprised to discover myself to be your mother, hovering off to one side to watch, in amazement, your marvellous transformation into the person you've become. In both cases, I am so very honoured to be included in your life, my love. You are a source of such great pride and joy to me, Kenya. The girl I used to be; the girl I never was.

To say it's difficult for me to believe that eight years have come and gone since you arrived would be an understatement of phenomenal proportions. When you were just born, eight-year-olds were foreign, faraway creatures. I could imagine being mother to one then about as well as I could imagine being mother to a seventeen-year-old today. (But I've learned my lesson now, and am steeling myself for any eventuality.)

It's in the night, my love, when I come closest to remembering how we began our journey together. That's when, at last, you're still. When the shrillness has subsided; when the frenzied activity has stopped. In their place, I find a lovely young lady, her coltish legs tangled up in the duvet, her hair a storm across the pillow. And somewhere in the silence, I recall the squalling infant she left behind. I remember the sweet-faced baby, nodding off in the stroller on our summertime walks around the block; the charming toddler, so obsessed with *Sleeping Beauty* it was the only video she'd watch; the perfect little girl, earnestly building the season's first snowman.

But the truth is, by the glow of the tiny Christmas lights we've draped across your shutters, I watch your lovely features in repose — and struggle to remember very much at all.

It's as inconceivable as it is heartbreaking to me to realize that what I have left of your early journey through childhood are only moments. Fluttering remnants which got snagged upon the branches of my mind only because they were remarkable in some way, like your first birthday at the indoor playground, or the thing you told Daddy when your new sister was born. And no matter how intensively I peer into the photos lining our walls, I cannot deny that the memories the images stir in me are thin. Surely I can remember what happened after I snapped that picture of you making Kool-Aid on the kitchen floor? Or the time you and Daddy lay at the bottom of the stairs in sunglasses, and giggled up at me and my camera leaning over the balcony? (You were still in diapers then. Amazing!)

But honestly I can't. All of those moments have accumulated on the other side of the wall. And too much time has passed for me to hoist myself over for a peek.

So I drink you up today, my eight-year-old marvel, and will my mind to make the impressions stick. I think of the everyday minutiae of your existence: you and Malindi stealing the huge cardboard box Daddy was threatening to put in recycling, and hiding it in your closet; the way you said the Grinch's Cindy Lou Who reminds you of Kai; how you lost your tiny dog figurine three separate times over lunch (how you ever get through the day, my dreamy darling, I do sometimes wonder). I want today (and tonight, with your soft-breathing, winter-night loveliness filling my senses) to populate my mental memory tree with vivid life. And I want that tree replanted on this side of the wall.

AULD LANG SYNE

Way back in the recesses of my childhood, I remember a New Year's Eve that has stayed spectacularly imprinted on my brain ever since. It was memorable for the fact that I was actually allowed to welcome midnight in real time. My first all-nighter. I must have been all of six years old, and I remember my parents were having a party in the living room. My seven-year-old brother Michael and I were determined that year to see the new year in with all the grownups. Better still, my best friends Penny and Wendy, twins who lived across the street, had been granted the same access.

When midnight struck, all of the kids spilled out onto the street in our pyjamas, clanging pots and pans together and basically making terrible nuisances of ourselves. Looking back now with a parent's perspective, I wonder what the inhabitants of the surrounding quiet households must have thought of our ragtag late-night celebration. But from the eyes of a child, I can confirm that it was priceless.

Later, New Year's Eves took on a different hue. The thought of hanging out with the big people — especially one's parents — became an increasingly ghastly concept, and the pressure mounted to make it a night to remember. One year, I remember charging in with a bunch of other teenagers on the party of some twelve-year-olds who had posted signs around the neighbourhood advertising that their parents would be gone for the evening. Strangely, we swiped some frozen raspberries from their basement freezer and left without saying goodbye. I remember a New Year's party when I was in first-year university in which I introduced my new boyfriend to my old high-school friends. We plundered the host's father's liquor cabinet, took to the great outdoors for snow angels at midnight and made prank calls to our old high-school teachers. The night ended with my escort and me getting his dad's van stuck in a snowbank on the side of a country road.

But once you have kids, the season of such tomfoolery must draw to a close. For one, it's suddenly a family holiday again. For another, if you think for a moment that you can hold on to your reputation as the Margarita Mistress who can out-limbo the best, well, you're setting yourself up for some sensational disappointment. Instead, you might dust off your Perry Como, rent *Old Yeller* and tuck up in bed when the kids do so you'll be fresh for waffles and tobogganing in the morning.

Not better. Not worse. Just different. Or so you have to keep telling yourself.

In fact, we endeavour to taste both worlds in our New Year's efforts. From early on, we've had a tradition of spending the evening with friends who are similarly endowed with offspring. Across the din of melting-down children, we bellow one-liners to each other until we're just too tired to bother anymore and someone flips on *Dick Clark*. The kids' energy almost always outlasts ours, and, by the end, we're so short-tempered and hopped up on sparkling grape juice it's all we can do to mutter a few perfunctory salutations upon the striking of the midnight bell before loading everyone in the minivan and heading for home.

But on the first day of each new year, when I wake — clear-headed — to a household of my babies and their exuberance over the antics in which they were allowed to participate the night before, I know one thing: New Year's Eve is every bit as memorable as it ever was. Not better. Not worse. Just different.

A NOTE OF HOPE

Dear Tooth Fairy, the letter we found under her pillow began. How are you? I am fine. I hope you are fine too. I have lost a tooth. Please take it and leave me some money. I have some questions too. What is your real name? Do you have any children? Where do you live? Thank you very much. And what do you do with all of those teeth? From Kenya.

Creeping around in the darkness, having surfaced from an almost-sleep with a jolt of memory about a little girl and the expectation of a visit from a certain dental sprite, I came across this hopeful missive. It was more than we'd bargained for, but I was delighted to find it just the same.

When Kenya had come to me to present her tiny bloody treasure earlier in the day, I'd realized her tooth wasn't all she'd lost. "I'm not going to put this under my pillow tonight," she'd told me in very deliberate tones. "I don't believe in the tooth fairy anymore."

I must admit, I've always been a bit ambivalent about the tooth fairy thing. Perpetuating the existence of the big fat guy who squeezes into a red suit every winter is exhausting enough, I find. And don't even get me started on the Easter Bunny.

But her skepticism here still caught me off guard. It's too soon, I thought, to lose the faith. So I grabbed Kenya's hand and chased after the big parental myth bus, which was just backing out of the station without my eldest child on it. And I pulled us both on board.

Convincing Kenya that maybe, just maybe, there *is* an elfin creature who races about the world stealing kids' lost teeth from under their pillows was not too tough a sell, after all. It quickly became apparent that my little girl still wanted to believe. She just needed a little nudge back into that space. In the end, as it turned out, I gave such a forceful nudge that she decided to take the whole deal to the next level, and to probe for details.

"She's got questions," I whispered to Adam. He squinted up at me hovering over the bed, a scrap of paper clutched in my hand.

"She wrote a letter to the tooth fairy, and we need to answer her questions," I said.

"Just leave her a dollar and let her think the tooth fairy was too busy to respond," he muttered.

I turned on the light. "No way," I said. If Kenya had been inquisitive enough to put together a list of clever questions for this tooth-obsessed gnome, we were going to take the time to address them. The kids know my writing much better than their father's, so Adam was elected the official respondent. I brought him a pen and a piece of paper.

I dug through my wallet as he wrote, and found three quarters and a pair of dimes. It would have to do. I got a Baggie from the kitchen to contain the coins and returned to our bedroom just as Adam was putting the finishing flourishes on what turned out to be a highly creative letter. He had told Kenya, in shaky block letters that would be sure to take her off her parents' trail, that his real name was Dentifrice, that he had no children, that he made fancy necklaces from his collection of teeth and that he lived in the city of Fluoride. I folded up the note and slipped it under Kenya's pillow with the money.

The next morning, we heard a commotion rising from across the hall. It was, I realized with surprising relief, the sound of a little girl rediscovering her faith.

A MOTHER DIVIDED

Downstairs, Leah, our wonderful babysitter, is sharing bits and pieces of my children's lives. I hear her, from my second-floor-office post, indulging their questions, fulfilling their requests, entertaining their whimsical observations of the world. As for me, I am nowhere to be seen.

This is a choice I have made. Unlike my friends who forsook their careers when their babies arrived, I have determined to both have a job and be a mommy, inconceivable though that may seem. It's a ridiculous notion, really, seeing how each is a full-time pursuit in its own right. And considering, too, that one shouldn't have children lightly, that one should be prepared to commit extensive energy and attention to the business of raising them. But I want other things in my life than just my kids. And I chase away the possibility that this is a selfish conceit like it was a fly around my face.

I catch myself, often, in silence, straining to hear what book Leah is reading them, or to decipher what craft project they've undertaken at the dining room table. Sometimes, it's all I can do not to charge down the stairs and into their midst, to take my place among them and let their energy swirl around me, little eddies of crazy love that catch me up and pull me under. It's especially hard to stay rooted when one of my children is hurt: when a jagged fragment of their pain, or a wail whose particular tone I recognize as one of genuine despair, escapes up the stairs. Instead, I let Leah tend to their suffering and flip open an e-mail to momentarily drown out the blood pounding in my ears; to squash the feverish guilt rising in my throat.

Because how could a woman not be with her babies? How could she lurk outside their lives, even for just a few hours at a time, and indulge in purely self-centred occupations? How could she, after painting the nursery, enduring the labour and filling the bookcase with smart books, choose, after all, to have a life of her own, too? How could she ever let someone else console and love her offspring in her stead, and still call herself a mother? How indeed.

The moment passes. And I have succeeded once again in convincing myself that it never even existed. Nor did the magical instant when a laughing Finn discovered the manic behaviour of a crazily deflating balloon in the downstairs hallway. Or when Kai took her first bouncy, circuitous piggyback ride on her big sister Kenya's back. Because I was not there to witness them. When I come downstairs at the end of the day, I will give Finn another balloon, and I will invite Kenya to put Kai on her back once more. Because if I am to survive this choice I've made, if I am to rise to the challenge of the thoughtful, engaged modern woman, I must believe that my children's most meaningful living takes place with me in it.

Lessons Learned Late

Youth, they say, is wasted on the young. I'd like to introduce my own variation to that parable: first babies are wasted on new mothers.

Here's where I'm going with this. When you have your first child, it's all uncharted ground. Every obstacle is encountered and overcome for the first time. Your kid doesn't sleep, doesn't eat, doesn't poop. He has gook coming out of his eye, he's losing his hair and sometimes his excretions are so forceful they reach the nape of his neck. All is fodder for the worry mill, and so new mothers spend half their time in paroxysms of consternation when really they should be sipping daiquiris and checking out the sidewalk sales.

Trust me. Kenya was a problem baby. Nobody can argue with me there. She had colic and cradle cap and everything in between. The only way to relieve her relentless twilight wailing was to lift her up and down under doorframes. She didn't sleep through the night till she was almost three, by which time her father and I were about ready to throw in the parenting towel. I often wonder whether her problems were feeding our anxieties or vice versa, but it was a trying time in any case.

Looking back on it now though, from the vantage point of fourth-child mayhem, I see the whole ordeal through different eyes.

One fresh-to-the-world little baby is a breeze. No bigger than a laptop and just as portable, a newborn isn't any more troublesome than a blister. Sure, she cries from time to time, but stick a boob in her mouth and you can generally get on with your day (so long as your day can unfold with an exposed breast in it). New babies sleep almost constantly. You can strap them onto your chest and be off with you. Movies, travel, whatever: the world is your oyster when you're sharing it with just a single child. But here's the crime: you don't realize all of this until it's too late; until your first baby is jamming toys into your VCR, and your second is screeching upstairs in the bassinette. You'll never have just one infant again — and you forgot to take advantage of it when you did.

Sweet baby Kai is a joy. She wants nothing more from life than a comfy place to lay her downy little head, an easy-to-access engorged breast and the occasional opportunity to swing in her fancy Fisher-Price contraption. As for me, experience has taught me that my infant's crying bouts will ebb and that the heat rash that sprang up on her chest today will be gone tomorrow. I know that babies are supposed to get gassy, and that pink eye is not a serious affliction. All of this means I enjoy her more and that my life is not anywhere near as stressed-out as it was when Kenya was a wee one.

But all of this wisdom is worthless now that I've added three more kids to the tribe. The best I can do at this point? Press it on my pregnant-with-their-first friends, and insist that they take advantage of the relative freedom of the early weeks and months of life with a firstborn. I wish I had.

To Kai, at Age One

Dear Kaikoura Grace,

How could it be that a year has passed since you first exploded into our lives? Surely it was only last month when I made that early-morning trip to the drug store, sheepishly avoiding the cashier's eyes as I laid my pregnancy test kit on the counter, and then slinking home to perch on the edge of my bathtub to read the double-line news. Later, I would announce it to your father from within the noisy security of a Ukrainian festival at the end of our street, and he would receive it with such knee-jerk joy that my heart would sing. (The cold reality of our situation would sink in soon enough.)

Surely it was only last week when the mountains of pain in my belly distracted me from that cheesy late-night movie and insisted we make the middle-of-the-night call to your grandparents to report that, at last, this was It. We asked if they could come on over to stay with your sisters and brother while we raced through the empty streets to the hospital, but then sat a half hour in the chilly kitchen with them before leaving, eating bowls of cereal and confirming that the contractions were closing in.

And surely it was only yesterday that you emerged into the world, hours later than I thought a fourth child would arrive, but still in time to catch the playoff hockey game on our little birthing suite TV. You were bigger than the others had been, but still looked so tiny in that little square Plexiglas container they rolled up beside my bed. I couldn't believe it when they told me your weight.

The year has passed so fluidly, my little girl, that it's difficult for me to put my finger on any one milestone that you've left in your wake. Looking back, I can scarcely remember the fleecy-of-hair, heavy-of-head, tucked-up-of limbs baby I tended to so lovingly in those first days and weeks. With three other children in our lives, it's such a luxury to have any private time to share with you, and I do remember the peacefulness of snuggling into bed to nurse you to sleep when all the others were finally quiet. But even that is less a concrete memory than a feeling. A feeling of bliss. A feeling of intimacy. A feeling of love.

A year into the game, I can see that you're going to give us a run for our money, sweet Kai. You're a loud, insistent little kid, who likes to exercise her vocal cords and can definitely hold her own in a screaming competition with her older siblings. You don't walk yet, but can scuttle about the place like a determined scorpion and find purchase on almost anything for cruising. I truly believe that the moment when you forget to hold onto my fingertips and take your first independent steps is only days away.

You're smart as a whip, my little Belle. I can't remember the other kids knowing any recognizable words at this age, but you can say "Mommy" like a pro and I'm pretty sure you've got "Daddy" locked up, too. And then there's "cat," the word you were delighted to discover represents those baby-sized creatures that wrap themselves around your legs. Hell, you think the word works just as well for any furry animal. I imagine it will take us a while to disabuse you of that notion.

And so the one-year mark that so alarmingly appeared on the horizon for a mother anxious about the day when there would be no more babies has receded into the distance. And here you lie, snoring on my bed. Your hair is wild, your fists are clenched. I love you like crazy, sweet last child. It's hard to believe that a year has passed since you first exploded into our lives.

SURVIVING THE SPLIT

Friends of ours, friends we have known since our firstborns were itty-bitty babies together, are splitting up. To Adam and me, sitting on the edges watching the carnage, it's a devastating situation. We are separate from their pain and activity — but intimately tied in, too.

Sheila and her husband Rick, and Adam and I took our first tastes of parenthood together. Their daughter Claire is exactly one month older than Kenya. Their boys Max and Tom are two months older than Malindi.

For years, the four parents would spend every weekend together, laughing like idiots over the heads of an increasing number of children in one or the other of our living rooms. We were shell-shocked — but at least we were shell-shocked together.

When Sheila and Rick raced off to the hospital after Sheila's water broke with the twins, Adam and I looked after Claire. When we picked nursery schools and tot programs for our babies, we always did so in tandem. Sheila and I have been each other's emergency contact persons for as far back as it's mattered.

For the first little bit though, I didn't know Sheila at all. I was aware only that a woman in the house three doors down had had a baby a few weeks before me. But then, just before Christmas eight years ago, with my baby in a Snugli and my arms filled with groceries from a local trip, I knocked on her door and invited her to help me form a mothers' group.

We've been inseparable ever since. For the longest time, weekend days would start with one of us finding a reason to drop in on the other. And then the morning would drift into afternoon, and the afternoon into evening. "What shall we order for dinner?" someone would eventually say, and we would laugh and laugh.

I remember a hundred moments from our lives as young parents. Mostly, they are tableaux, images frozen against a backdrop of the rich, complicated experience of becoming a mother. Casting back through them, I see the girls, just learning to sit up, surrounded by toys and facing each other on a blanket in Sheila's living room. I hear our sober conversations about bedtimes and routine and the wonders of Tempra. I see Kenya and Claire sharing baths and sprinkler sprints and birthday cakes. I remember the endless cavalcade of Barney videos, and see the four of us adults, perched on the couch watching them for several minutes before somebody would point out that the kids had left for another room.

And I see the walks, hundreds of them, around and around that block that marked the boundary of our existence as young mothers. Sheila would wait for me at the end of my path, rocking her triple stroller up and down, feeding the boys Cheerios and adjusting their canopies as I hauled my double down from the porch. Our mommy years are all tangled up in each other.

But this unexpected event has combed the tangles into separate strands. And I find myself totally unprepared for it. As much as your logical mind recognizes the absurdity of it, there's an unspoken assumption that the support system you install in your life when your kids arrive will always be there. Having it disintegrate is totally unnerving.

Now Adam and I will frequently find ourselves at odds on weekend days that we might otherwise have whiled away in the company of our similarly offspring-burdened pals. How sad to have been abandoned. How strange to be picking up the next stage of the parenting years on our own.

Sheila and I will always be friends, and so will our children. She is my cherished confidante and Claire is Kenya's greatest treasure. But our little band is no more. Our bleary-eyed mutual introduction to the hilarities and hysterics of being a parent will stand as an episode, frozen in time. I'll miss them — along with the younger, less jaded version of us — and all that we embodied of the magic of new parenthood.

THE MIRACLE OF GRANDPARENTS

"I love you too, Grandma," says Kai, into the portable phone I hold against her ear. When I try to pull it away, she gets anxious and insists on having it back so she can share the same sentiments with her grandfather. How wonderful, I think, for all of them.

My parents are nobody's idea of the typical grandparents. They're still just sixty, and full of vim. My mom's so young looking no one can believe she's a grandma, and my dad's an all-guns-blazing self-employed lawyer who will never retire. I love that they're still dynamic enough to play a big part in my kids' lives. A grandparent's imprint on a child's development is wildly different from a parent's. Plus, they always have ice cream in their freezer.

I have extremely fond memories of my own grandparents. I remember playing leapfrog on the lawn outside my dad's mother's house, and visiting the menagerie of four-legged creatures my mom's mother always kept (and still does keep). My grandpa, who died when I was not quite fourteen, was such a star in my eyes. He made jokes I didn't understand (and then winked at me) and bought me a new bike at the cottage every year. My nana was (and continues to be) the coolest lady around. She wore leather pants, let me stand between her legs while we took the hills in her Volkswagen and bounced on the hotel beds right along with us.

My parents, once they got over the initial shock of realizing they were about to be somebody's grandparents, could not wait for my babies to be born. In the months leading up to Kenya's grand entrance, my mother and I would make daily telephone contact, to ponder the evolving state of my fetus and to dream about her arrival. When I finally went into labour, they rode the roller coaster right along with us, and arrived at the hospital mere minutes after Kenya did.

Ever since, Grandma and Boppa (Kenya could never quite handle "Grandpa") have embraced their new roles with all the enthusiasm I had hoped they would. They followed us to this neighbourhood shortly after Kenya was born, and we see each other at least a couple of times a week. On Tuesday evenings, after I drop Malindi at Sparks, Kenya comes with me for a special visit with them. There, she gets to bask in her grandparents' undivided attention, to share the bread and butter they're having with their dinner and to spin her little eight-year-old yarns for two people who hang on her every word.

Thursday mornings are Grandma time for Malindi. Some months ago, family consensus determined that this little five-year-old was the child most in need of nurturing, at least at this point in our family's development. And so Malindi Mornings were born. Grandma dedicates half her day off to junk-art crafts and kitchen-table book publishing. She feeds Malindi lunch and even drops her at school.

Occasionally, my parents will give Adam and me a night off. They'll come by after work and we'll order everybody a pizza before making our escape. They'll watch *Finding Nemo* with the kids, and read them stories. They won't brush their teeth ("I don't do teeth," my mom will say), but that only makes their presence even more adored.

The next day, the phone will ring at our house. It will be Grandma or Boppa just calling to chat with one of the children.

"We miss them," they'll say. It's always this way. They come off a hit of the grandkids just aching for more. I love that.

"I'll go get Kai," I'll tell them. When I've got her, I'll hold the phone up to her ear.

To the Hospital

It's midnight on a very cold night, and I'm still hours from sleep. In another pocket of the city, three of my babies snuggle under their duvets and dream in a household full of love. But Malindi lies beside me in a hospital emergency room cot. For us it's been a nightmare.

We've been here for hours, she and I, me trying to distract her from her discomfort with well-worn waiting-room storybooks and games of I Spy with the big wall mural. Intermittently, a member of the medical staff will pay us a visit, to take Malindi's temperature and poke her belly. Each time they do, she stares up at me in silence, and her big brown eyes fill with tears. They had to take blood, too, a wrenching ordeal that choked the pediatrics ward with my little girl's screams.

At last, the patient has fallen asleep. I take off her boots and tuck a blanket around her tiny, pain-wracked body.

Malindi and I came to the hospital because the aches in her gut were so severe, doubling her over and making her vomit, that Adam and I became convinced it was nothing less than appendicitis. I'd grabbed several changes of pyjamas, Malindi's simian sleep-buddy, Monkster, and a magazine for me. Several hours in, I've finished my magazine and we're no closer to a diagnosis.

"Has she gone pee yet?" an abrasive nurse asks, storming into our room and flipping on the lights. Malindi and I have endured several unsuccessful trips to the bathroom across the hall, her wincing in agony on the toilet, me pleading with her to *please go pee.* "Nope," I say. "And I don't want to put her through that again."

"Then we'll have to catheterize the kid," the dreadful nurse says, plucking at her words so that they're delivered to me as the only fitting punishment for my having been unable to convince my child to urinate. She draws a curtain around our bed.

"No, Mommy, no!" Malindi yelps, when she realizes what is about to take place.

"I'm sorry, sweetie," I whisper into her ear, and I wrap my body around her arms to contain them. Further down the bed, two nurses pin her legs open and insert a tube into her urethra.

"No!" Malindi screams. "No!"

"It's OK," I whisper again and again. My tears drop into her hair. At last, it's over.

I turn out the lights and my terrified little girl is released from the grip of modern medicine. "Mommy," she says, her huge, wet eyes locking on mine. "That hurt."

"I know," I say. "I know."

I smooth back her hair and kiss her eyelids and stroke her cheek until, still shuddering with residual sobs, she sleeps again. In the morning, after an ultrasound has revealed that Malindi does not have appendicitis, and a process of deduction has concluded that her discomfort is the result of a treatable urinary tract infection, we will be released. But tonight, I will climb into the bed beside my daughter, and gingerly position myself on the narrow mattress so I don't disturb her slumber. I will wrap my arm around her tender, wounded belly, and lie there a while, remembering the last time we shared a hospital bed together, the night she was born. This is what it is to be a mommy, I will think: perching on the edge of a bed, listening to the laboured breathing of your babies and wishing, somehow, to take away their pain.

The Attraction of Mommy

In my house, I am a kid magnet. Everywhere I go, the kids follow. They are sniffer dogs, and I am the target hare.

From time to time, they have very specific needs that make them seek me out (Open that drawer, Help me with my piano, Let me nurse). But, more often than not, these junior members of my family just want the reassurance of my physical presence. They want to know that I'm at their disposal, should they require me. I am their 9-1-1.

Sometimes, certainly, it's wonderful to be wanted. How sad it would be to flicker through your life without anyone ever fighting over who gets to sit next to you, or gets to hold your hand when you cross the street. But catch me in the wrong space, and I'll give you a very different opinion. After all, sometimes a person just wants to have a bath without being asked to wipe someone's bum.

What happened at our house last night was a perfect illustration of my magnetic personality in action. The kids had just finished leftover chili and, with radioactive orange gunk still smushed around their mouths, were starting to dissipate. Kenya was lying on the floor in the dining room, singing a song she'd learned at Brownies called "I'm Going to Tell on You." Malindi was chasing Finn around and around a well-worn loop through the rooms of the first floor, leaping clumsily over their big sister whenever they encountered her. Kai was in the kitchen, categorizing the cans in the lower cupboard. As for me, I was — always in their sight — clearing the table and washing the dishes and daydreaming about Viggo Mortenson.

It had been an extraordinarily long day. Both older girls had had piano after school, an exercise which involves much to-ing and fro-ing with a quartet of children. Despite the fact that the teacher lives just up and across our street, I still have to haul every last one of my offspring on each drop-off and pick-up.

While Kenya was in her lesson, Malindi had wanted me to "play animals" with her (an oft-repeated request whose fulfilment involves considerable injury to the kneecaps and the sustainment of verbal defamation from "the owner"). While Malindi was in her lesson, I had run through Kenya's dictée words with her, and endured much backlash for mispronouncing *beaucoup de* French words. Throughout, I was getting dinner ready, entertaining Finn's demands to measure parts of the house and his person with his new measuring tape, and lugging Kai around in my arms.

And so it was that when Adam burst into our harried midst just after six, it was all I could do not to rush past him and hurry out the door in the other direction (possibly not stopping until I'd reached Fiji). He needs time to acclimatize, I'm always reminding myself. So, instead of screaming, I warbled, "How was your day?" into the front hall.

Soon, though, after he had changed his clothes and checked the mail and dropped the newspaper in the recycling box, he was mine. And they were his.

"I think I'm going to have a bath," I said. Adam, bless his heart, was all in favour of my plan. But he was no more in a position to make it a reality than I was. First, I tried to hand him Kai and duck out. Her responding despair was too much for me to bear, though, and so I took her back. Eventually I earned her trust enough to put her down on the family room floor with some Lego. But when I tried to tiptoe out of view, she spied me, and the wails began again.

Eventually, I did escape. I made it upstairs and ran myself a bath and enjoyed its soothing effects for almost two-and-a-half glorious minutes. And then the sniffer dogs found me.

The rumble of children rising up a case of stairs has a sound like a brewing storm. It grows ever louder until it's outside a door, its forceful pressure threatening to blow its hinges. When it arrives, quick action is required.

Last night, when it blew up on me, I pressed my hand against the pressure from the outside just in time, and kept a visiting Finn at bay. "Mommy's having a bath," I hollered through the door. He couldn't have cared less.

A few minutes later, during which I had turned up the faucets to drown out the hallway noise, and was starting to think Finn might have given up the ghost, I noticed his measuring tape snaking under the door crack. And then Kenya and Malindi arrived, too, and they pushed the door open before I could catch it. Kai, who'd been screaming on its other side for the past several minutes, jumped at the opportunity and raced into the bathroom. I put down my magazine and reached for the towel. All was lost.

In the end, I gave over my warm asylum to a horde of inmates who were already slipping out of their clothes in anticipation of sharing it. It's nice to be wanted, I told myself, as I flopped down on the bed. But I didn't get to reflect on it for long: In no time, I was joined by four shivering children, dripping bathwater onto my bedroom carpet and demanding towels.

THE SCOURGE

The lousy affair began more than two weeks ago, when one of Kenya's very closest friends discovered she had head lice. The news arrived via telephone: Ashmir's mother felt duty bound to spread the word, especially in light of the fact that Kenya and Malindi had recently had a sleepover with the victim. I knew something was up, from Adam's long silences and the way his face lost its colour. Ashmir's got lice, he announced, when he hung up, and then followed on with a string of obscenities fit for the ears of neither child nor louse. For Kenya, he was convinced, it was only a matter of time.

Sure enough, a few days later, the scourge surfaced *chez nous.* I don't believe a person ever forgets her first louse. For me, the burned-in-the-brain image is the sight of a terrible brown beast, creeping its way across my oldest daughter's scalp as she hunched over the sink. In the bright light of the bathroom, the truth (long suspected in view of the extraordinary itchiness of her head) was revealed.

The next morning, armed with an abundance of Internet-based intelligence and "the best lice comb on the market," we started in on the ordeal. I bagged up every furry friend in my daughters' room. Even the dolls, their matted hair an open invitation for pest accommodation, were banished to garbage-bag exile. All of these sacks I dragged down to the front porch, much to the wailing despair of their contents' owners.

Next, I hauled clothes — every last piece — out of my daughters' dresser drawers, and delivered them down to the basement. This would be the "clean room" for our lice-eradication enterprise. Over the next three days, with the considerable assistance of our tireless babysitter, Leah, I washed and dried all of the garments, and cleared the cellar shelves to set up temporary holdings for them. I also stripped the beds and laundered the sheets and duvet covers in hot water. I put the duvets and pillows into the dryer for half an hour a pop. That would be enough to scald any critters clinging to the bedclothes for salvation.

In between loads, I vacuumed the entire house, with particular emphasis on the sleeping quarters. We lifted the mattresses off the beds and rolled back the slats. If any louse had wafted down to the carpet, he was now the victim of a powerful sucking hose.

By the time Adam arrived home in the late afternoon, I was exhausted. But the delousing business was only just beginning.

We must have looked ridiculous, the four of us, gathered in our living room on that Friday evening. Kenya and Malindi sat in front, their hair freshly dampened, wearing only towels (everything else was being washed!). We had rented some crappy kids' movie, and put out a bowl of pretzels, in the hopes that we might actually distract them from the arduous goings-on behind them. Adam and I sat in the rear, each of us with white sheets safety-pinned around our necks. The sheets extended to our daughters, and were wrapped around their shoulders and fastened under their chins. The purpose of this get-up, we had been informed, was to catch and identify any beasties that the combing-out process unloosed.

We doused the girls' heads with a combination of conditioner and cider vinegar that had me craving fish and chips all night, and then started the two-hour operation of dragging the steel comb through their hair. With a mixture of pure horror and lurid fascination, we would inspect the incredibly finely spaced teeth after each drag. By the end of the night, we'd found four lice on each girl (each of which we dutifully drowned in a bowl of water that was eventually flushed down the toilet). We may have found nits, too, but were extremely underconfident about our ability to identify the tiny eggs.

Then we slopped a mess of olive oil on their heads, packaged them up in shower caps and sent them to bed.

We rinsed and repeated this operation for the next two nights, including Finn and Kai the second night (the former was clear; the latter was not). After the kids would go to bed — smelling like salad dressing and staining their pillowcases all the while — Adam would comb me. In a fit of pique, I had aided the process by rushing outside with a Samurai ponytail on top of my head, and chopped the entire thing off. More than a foot of hair, still bound by elastic, dropped to the earth.

On the third day, we called in a delousing expert. We were worried about overlooked nits, and wanted an all-clear so we could send the girls back to school on Monday. The nice man, who arrived with elaborate headgear (magnifying goggles and a high-intensity lamp) and a fifty-five-dollar-an-hour price tag, spent four hours parsing through our family's follicles. He even gave my parents, who had been experiencing sympathetic itching, a once-over.

I've never seen a family do such a thorough job, he said, as he came up empty, again and again. In the end, he found one tiny nit in Kenya's hair, and another in Malindi's. But it was remarkable to find so little, he praised. We glowed with a curious, unfamiliar pride. Then he gave us a prescription for follow-up care (olive oil every four days for twelve days; a comb-through once a week for the rest of the school year) and his bill.

Since then, we've gradually been transporting articles of clothing back into the kids' drawers. And we've allowed the return of a handful of special stuffed sleepmates to their bedroom. But we still send Kenya to school with a garbage bag, to pack her coat and hat in, lest they mix with infested counterparts in the cloakroom. And our front porch continues to look like a war was waged there.

But if a battle has been fought, we are the victors. The lice we hosted, long since committed to the city's septic system, are defeated. For now. The lice expert advises us that it would be naive to expect never to encounter the enemy again. In the meantime, I shall never forget my first.

TIE BREAKING

The day when my sweet baby Kai and I will no longer share an intimate connection that has bound us since she emerged from my belly looms large. Sometime soon, I fear, she and I will have to wean: her from me and me from her.

For almost two years now, I have regularly invoked the official wisdom of the World Health Organization — which recommends that babies be breastfed for their first two years. Indeed, it has become my mantra in the face of those for whom the sight of a mother breastfeeding a child any bigger than a wee infant is so uncomfortable that they simply cannot hold their tongues.

The individuals whose tongues have not been held are sometimes surprising. Certainly I expected disapproval from my grandmothers, who think the practice obscene and will not hesitate to question the presumed lascivious nature of my motivation to keep it up. But not from my mother, who has done an exemplary job of restraining herself in most aspects of her daughter's child-rearing choices. She betrays her position on this one, though, by discharging an involuntary sigh of disdain when she sees me — once again — unbuttoning my shirt to comfort my distraught child. Even Adam, who supports me in all of my most personal maternal choices, asks, from time to time: When are you weaning her again?

Truth to tell, I wish I didn't have to. I wish there wasn't a timetable dictating our actions. I wish I'd never brought up the two-year deadline, and that we could play our loving ritual out to its natural conclusion.

From the start, my daughter's relationship with my breasts was well defined. When she was new, I nursed her constantly, and she drank of me with a vengeance. I was surprised by how much it hurt, in spite of her lovely latch and my considerable experience. Indeed, it surprised me to find myself breaking the suction with relief, and replacing my nipple's place in her pucker with a rubber pacifier.

Eventually though, the pain subsided, as it always had before with my previous children. My nipples took on an indifferent leatheriness and my baby's constant suckling became a given. She cried for my breasts intermittently through the night, and insisted upon nursing at frequent intervals during the day. When she could crawl, she made a beeline for my lap. When she could talk, she invented a word we both knew meant breast-time. Eventually, she learned to walk right on over, position herself across my legs and yank up my shirt.

Today, at twenty months, Kai recognizes her mother's occasional weariness with the request. More? I'll ask, and she'll laugh and assume the position. She says hello to my breast, when she reveals it. Sometimes, she'll say goodbye, and flip my shirt back down. But it's just a game: we both know she wouldn't give up the breast that easily.

Indeed, my breasts have become an open bar for Kai, who lounges beneath them in her glory, leisurely unfurling her body to observe her siblings at play, and then tucking back in for another long draw at the teat. It is her pleasure that my breasts always be made available, day and night. I might as well have a "We never close" sign installed across my sternum.

I've heard that some babies wean themselves, but that seems a fantastic notion at this stage with Kai. I can't remember much of how the breastfeeding chapters drew to a close with my other three, but I don't think I anticipated the kind of trauma I know will accompany this one. Mind you, I don't believe any of the others were as attached to the practice as number four is.

Just the same, I am already preparing for the finale. I will often try and distract Kai, when she comes to root. I'll suggest we watch a cartoon, or I'll produce a book or I'll plonk her in front of me on the couch to sing "Itsy Bitsy Spider." But the ploys have yet to work. This baby knows my game, and she's having none of it.

And so the breastfeeding continues. If there's company about when Kai makes a move, I'll sigh very publicly in response, for best effect. But my true feelings aren't hard to discern. I love nursing my little baby as much as she loves to be nursed. And the thought of breaking this sweet connection — during which I drink her in as much as she does me — is simply too hard to swallow.

THE PARK

At the top of our street is a patch of green with a dirt clearing in the middle. There are four swings there (two big-kid, two baby), three slides (two little, one long and steep), a climbing frame, a teeter-totter, monkey bars and a box of sand. It is the park, and it is the centre of our universe.

As soon as the ground thaws in the spring, and sunlight starts poking through the clouds, we're there. It's a sticky, soppy mess then, and so are we by the time we're making our way back home, but it's worth it to get a taste of the place again. Being back in its protective embrace makes a person, weary from too much winter, feel hopeful, even with its muck-filled wading pool, and the swing swamps that threaten to swallow up the children soaring above them. It's a reminder of what lies ahead: summers so warm that you have to spread your picnic blanket under the shade of a tree, the frisson of excitement that grips a person in response to the jingling approach of the ice cream truck, and freedom from the tyranny of school and work and weather.

And then from there, the park is a regular destination, playing host to our ragtag family almost daily. While school is still on, we turn right instead of left when we reach our street at the end of the day. Kenya dumps her knapsack in a heap beside the stroller and skips off to huddle with friends who have also made a park stop on their way home. Finn makes a dash for the swings, and Malindi begs me to play "chase" with her. "Park" was one of the first words baby Kai ever said.

By the time summer holidays take blessed hold, signalling the arrival of park water (to the wading pool and the drinking fountain), we are in a happy groove. Now this urban haven could host our family at any time of day. And it does: in bits and pieces in the early hours, as Leah takes the little ones for some air while I work; and then as a full unit, at the tail end of the sun's deliciously long tenure in the sky, when Daddy has returned home from the office.

We hold out at the park for as long as we can, gradually adding layers of clothing in accordance with the encroaching cold. We hang tougher than other families, who turn their backs on the oasis when the city yanks the lifeguard and drains the pool for the season. They used to unhitch the swings then, too, but someone must have pointed out that it's still as lovely to pump for the heavens with a down vest on as it is in a T-shirt, and so now they leave them dangling. Only when the snows fly, leaving frosty mounds at the base of the slides and making the icy swing chains sing in the wind, do we give up the park dream for another year, and retreat to the basement.

I believe that every childhood has a central location. It's a personal backdrop that sets the scene for your youth. It might be a schoolyard or a mall or the intersection of roads where you played Kick the Can every evening after dinner. And it's here that adults go whenever they summon up the years of their own faraway prime. I haven't a doubt that, for my four park-crazy kids, our little patch of green will be that place.

SQUANDERED CHANCES

My eight-year-old daughter Kenya is too old to play Candy Land. I realized that with soul-sucking sadness yesterday as I caught sight of the suggested age range on the cardboard box high in her closet. We didn't play it enough, she and I. And now it's too late.

When your babies are new, with fresh-from-the-bath hair and tiny feet you can tuck into terry sleepers, you believe there will be time for everything. With all the days and weeks and months and years to come, you can't imagine not fitting it all in. Painting a mural on your daughter's bedroom wall. Sewing clothes for her dolly. Taking her to the circus and the Ice Capades and Montreal.

But then you wake up one day and realize you didn't spend nearly enough Saturday mornings sharing colouring book spreads. Didn't paint enough Easter eggs at the kitchen table. Didn't have enough watergun fights or ever spend enough time teaching the art of squeezing cherry pits so they zing against the backyard fence. Suddenly, your babies are two, or six or sixteen, and the time for chalky sidewalk drawings has come and gone. You never did build them that playhouse or get much use out of the teaset Daddy brought home from his business trip. Now your daughter's too old to want to push her baby in a stroller beside you on a springtime walk. Too big to read the *Little House* books. Too distracted to collect pretty rocks at the beach. Too skeptical to expect any more visits from the Tooth Fairy.

"One day," I tell my children, about everything from visiting Disney World to learning to knit. But it's my great fear to wake up and realize that "one day" never came. We never did go go-karting. Or watch the sun rise together. Or camp out on our back deck. Or even bring Luther the dog in for show and tell.

Looking back from here, I realize I was naive. I didn't stop to consider that babies really only have a couple of round-bellied summers in them, kids just a handful of Santa Claus Christmases. Newborn diapers give way to size one, three and then five. Kindergarten becomes grade two, and grade two drifts into grade eight. Hard to imagine, but one day (soon) you'll squint into that picture of your sweet angel on Santa's knee and won't be able to remember if she was four or if she was five. Fat dimpled fingers will have lengthened, baby curls will have fluttered to the barber's floor and you'll take your child's face in your hands and marvel at the changes time has written across it. Such are the miracles and heartbreaks of parenthood. Such are the lessons that dawn on us all as we figure it out for ourselves.

So we must remember these teachings, especially on those dreadfully long days we spend in the company of our offspring. And we must treasure each time a little hand reaches for our own as we cross the street; every stroll to the park to share cheese strings and juice boxes; even the interminable layovers in the bathroom, balled-up tissue in hand, waiting for progress on the potty. And we must, too, for heaven's sake, squeeze in as many snowmen and shoulder rides and dandelion crowns and — yes — games of Candy Land as we possibly can.

BREAKING THE RULES

Someday, I swear, my head is going to explode. It won't be pretty. But neither is the occasional state of mind that results when my poisoned maternal brain tells me I'm worthless, worthless, worthless.

There's a rule in our house that only one person can cry at once. If Kai is already howling, Finn's not allowed to start. If Malindi's pitching a fit about the colour of her cereal bowl, Kenya cannot screech about her homework struggles. And so on. This afternoon, after a morning of spilling fruit punch on our pants and letting the guinea pig turn the family-room chair into his own personal toilet, the rule was cast out the window.

We were putting our coats on to take Malindi to school, and Kai spotted Luther's leash. I attached it to his collar only to keep the insistences that I do so at bay. I shouldn't have, because it just raised the kids' hopes (to say nothing of the dog's) that we were about to go out for a schnauzer walk. In the end, I broke up a fight between Finn and Kai about who was going to hold the leash with the announcement that neither of them would be holding it as Luther wasn't coming with us at all. And, furthermore, I said, I needed everybody out the door that instant or we were going to be even more late than we already were.

With that, I unhooked the dog, and yanked a screaming toddler and a collapsed-to-the-ground preschooler onto the front porch, banging my elbow on the doorframe and dropping my purse in the process. Getting Kai into her car seat was an exercise of pure muscle. She arched her back with such force, wailing with all her might throughout, that I had to lean my entire upper body into her to get the straps done up.

At the same time, Malindi and Finn were squabbling about whose feet were blocking whose entry into the van. The predicament was obstructing the sliding door. "Just get in," I barked.

Eventually, I got Malindi to school. Kai screamed the whole way there, and Finn brooded beside her. When I told him I was taking him to a babysitter for a couple of hours, he started to cry, as well. So much for the rule.

Coming out into the fresh air to release Malindi into the schoolyard was a sincere relief. My head was pounding, and I felt there was every possibility I might shriek into the sky. Instead, I told my sweet daughter I loved her, and waved goodbye.

Dropping Finn at Rita's is always bittersweet. It's nice for him, because it gives him a playmate, and a chance to visit at someone else's house. But it's awful, too, because he really just wants to hang out with his mommy, and I feel so miserable for not indulging this pure, simple, completely reasonable wish, that I want to throw up on the sidewalk on my way back to the car.

Instead, I climb in and try to convince Kai to stop crying, dammit. But she won't. And so I just turn on the radio and drive. I drive and I drive, and let my mind explore black thoughts, like my failure as a mother, and my utter uselessness at getting all the things in my life to work together well. I'm always pushing my kids away to work, or my work away to be with the kids. Ultimately, I despond, I'm doing neither thing well. I lose my patience with both worlds all the time. And my house is so extraordinarily unkempt that it would take a stick of dynamite to even get an edge.

On top of that, I haven't got any friends. I've got no time for exercise or reading or even washing my hair. And I certainly haven't the opportunity to prepare the nutritious meals I know my children should be eating. I've got so much on my plate that I'd need four of me to ever clear it. It's why my kids are always late for school, rarely have the proper footwear and are generally without their library books on library day. Mine are the scrawny, messy-haired children whose shabby appearances, I imagine, tell vast tales about the ineptitude of their mother.

These are the thoughts that swirl around my head as I drive my minivan in circles around the neighbourhood on this terrible day, willing my youngest child to please stop crying. Eventually, she does, and falls asleep.

Good thing, too: otherwise, I would have broken the rule.

THE SALVATION OF KAI

I think we're done. My mother will cluck her tongue, and my friends will shake their heads, but I really do think we're finished having children. And as much as it aches to have reached that conclusion, I must admit that I do so with a certain amount of relief.

After all, it's incredibly difficult to face the birth of friends' babies with trepidation, to regard all pregnant women with jealousy, to approach each new babe with a lump in your throat. At last, I feel I am over the procreation hump. I can hold a new infant in my arms, and celebrate all of her wonderfulness without having to suppress a yearning that threatens to tear my inner organs to shreds. And even though I have still occasionally been heard to whimper, "Let's have another," to Adam, I don't really feel the pull anymore (not that Adam ever receives the suggestion with much enthusiasm himself). My baby-bearing days are over.

Fortunately for me, though, I am not without a close-at-hand reference to all that is wonderful about babies.

Kaikoura Grace is our rose-coloured flourish on the cake; our little last utterance of fertility; our final boarding call from the departure lounge before the flight takes off.

And what a wonderful specimen with whom to enjoy the end of the trip. With her billowing furrow of silky auburn hair, her round little belly and her intense grey-blue gaze, she is a real live touchstone to "remember when," even as her blossoming siblings leave her in their wake. Like remember when our flailing-limbed babies shared our beds (until their scratchy little claws could be tolerated no longer). Or remember when babies slept (so vulnerably!) with their arms flung up over their heads and their feet turned out like ballerinas, mid-hop. Or remember when toddlers waved hello to airplanes and said I love you to teddy bears.

We treasure our last child for all that she represents of our entire quartet of children and because, for all the hustle-bustle, we can at last savour the pleasure of a baby. And what a lucky baby she is, to have three older siblings who will knock down the road blocks and pave a well-worn path for her.

Finn and Malindi and Kenya will not only test the waters for Kai, they'll teach her how to swim. And she'll have as many built-in playmates as built-in caregivers. Lovely Kaikoura, the last baby I will ever carry in my belly and push into the world, the last child who will ever join our club with an official card of membership, will always be cherished. She is, after all (this time I promise!), the sweet final punctuation mark to our run-on family.

FLEETING THOUGHTS

On September 7, Kenya will enter fourth grade, Malindi will start grade one, Finn will enter junior kindergarten and Kaikoura will start her first year of nursery school. That's little, tiny Kenya, who visited Costa Rica with us and saw her first toucan; who called Barney "Ba-Ba" and sat entranced in his presence; whose first trip to a babysitter left me a shattered mommy in the front seat of a car.

And little, tiny Malindi, who loved cake so much she made it one of her first words; who stayed up till midnight the New Year's she was one-and-a-half; who called pussycats "galldigaws" (because she couldn't pronounce the real thing) and sought them out around every corner.

And little, tiny Finn, whose flossy baby hair would bunch up in the back like the fronds of a palm tree; who would spin the toilet paper roll in cascading swaths of white onto the bathroom floor; whose love for fish and light switches and electric trains almost matched his love for Mommy.

And little, tiny Kai, who laughed before she smiled, sang before she talked, danced before she walked.

These are the babies I will release to the system.

Somewhere along the line, it seems, time got away from me.

Last night, Adam and I were relishing a rare moment of privacy at the kitchen table, and marvelling about how the experience of having children in your life forces you always to live in the present.

Neither of us can remember Kenya as the wee, limb-flailing infant my journals confirm that she was. We remember almost nothing of Malindi's or Finn's babyhoods. And even the memory of Kai, who isn't quite two, has dissolved like the fizzy bubbles that burst above a Fresca.

And yet, when we look on the kids as they exist today, we can't imagine that the moment won't forever be available for recall. After all, how could we ever forget that Finnie mispronounces "peacock" as "pea-cop" and "peanuts" as "pea-nups"? That Malindi gets lost in conniptions of indecision over which of her twin boyfriends she will marry? That Kenya is obsessed with knowing all the different breeds of dogs? And that baby Kai kisses the animal pictures in all of her board books?

But we will forget.

And we'll forget, too, the way Finn kept collections of everything, from batteries to keys to elastic bands. And how we waited for Kenya's front teeth to finally punch through her gums. And how Malindi had her own peculiar version of the alphabet. And how little Kai would say, "I love you, too" before anyone had even said a word about loving her.

Because the truth is, all of this is fleeting. And, before you know it, just as you're momentarily distracted by something on TV, just as you stoop down to tie a shoe or buckle up a car seat, just as you look up from folding the laundry, you'll be amazed to discover that time has swept by you like a wave. And your eight-year-old will be starting fourth grade, your almost-six-year-old will be going into grade one, your four-year-old will be entering kindergarten and your precious last-baby two-year-old will be going into nursery school.